Advance Praise

for *Biblical Eldership: Back to the Future with Spirit-Filled Leadership in the Local Church*

There's a huge army, a mature and able force within the church that is hitherto idle, a sleeping giant, if you will. *Biblical Eldership* is about activating the missing link in the functional structure of the church; it's about waking up the glorious army of Christ within His Church and giving them the platform and equipping to effectively fulfill the great commission. Being part of this project is of tremendous blessings to our church, it makes pastoring easier for me personally. I do recommend that every believer who is serious about fulfilling the Great Commission should get a copy and join forces with their local church leadership in raising Biblical Eldership in their local assembly.

Sam Adeyemi, Senior Pastor,
Overcomers Christian Center, Columbus, Ohio

Scott in his research has tackled one of the most significant leadership challenges the local church faces today. *Biblical Eldership* will change the way you lead and transform the leadership environment in your local congregation. You will raise the level of effectiveness, confidence, expectation and joy of your lay leaders when you implement Scott's Biblical template of investing in developing an Elder team.

By implementing Scott's *Biblical Eldership* template for training elders, I now have leaders who love the elder team meetings, have taken their understanding of shared community to a whole new level, and have significantly changed the leadership environment in our congregation. We really are doing ministry together.

Ray D. Hock, DMin., Pastor,
Bright Hope Fellowship, Middletown, Pennsylvania

Two years ago, I assembled a group of men under the inspiration and direction of Scott Kelso called "elders." Every week we meet and seek God together for direction, encouragement, and spiritual oversight. This group of men has become an invaluable part of the ministry that takes place at EUM Church. I treasure the time that I spend with them and cannot image doing ministry without their support and encouragement. I believe that assembling this team was one of the best decisions I made in my tenure as Lead Pastor of EUM Church.

Rev. Dr. Jeff Harper, Lead Pastor,
EUM Church, Greenville, Ohio

A few years ago, Dr. Kelso invited me, as his Doctor of Ministry dissertation advisor, to observe eleven elders ministering in a difficult counseling session. The men did not appear to be more or less than a cross-section of men from the community, but they operated with jaw-dropping spiritual insight and effectiveness. The cooperation, humility, and deference to each other and toward the counselees was breathtaking. I never thought that eleven "average" laymen could work together so smoothly and effectively toward a genuinely satisfactory outcome.

If I were skeptical that elders could function in this way, that skepticism was put to rest that afternoon. My recurring thought, as a professional minister and counselor, was, "These men are so incredibly well trained!" This experience lent great credibility to Dr. Kelso's project—the material you are about to read. I believe it works, not only because he developed a highly effective method for training church elders, but also because Kelso's method is grounded on the best grasp of the biblical principles that I have ever seen.

If the reader truly seeks to follow the central New Testament mandate to make disciples (in this case, elders), then *Biblical Eldership* is the place to start.

Dr. Jon Mark Ruthven, Professor Emeritus, Theology,
Regent University School of Divinity;
author, *On the Cessation of the Charismata* and
What's Wrong with Protestant Theology?

BIBLICAL ELDERSHIP

BIBLICAL ELDERSHIP

Back to the Future with
Spirit-Filled Leadership
in the Local Church

Scott Kelso, D.Min.

WORD & SPIRIT PRESS

Tulsa, Oklahoma USA

*Biblical Eldership: Back to the Future
with Spirit-Filled Leadership in the Local Church*

Copyright © 2016 by Scott Kelso, D.Min.

http://www.iceonfire.org/

All rights reserved. No part of this book may be reproduced or transmitted in any form or by any means, electronic or mechanical, including photocopying and recording, or by any information storage and retrieval system, without permission in writing from the publisher.

Published by Word & Spirit Press LLC, Tulsa, OK

http://WordandSpiritPress.com

ISBN 978-1-943489-01-5 softcover

ISBN 978-1-943489-02-2 electronic

Unless otherwise indicated, all Bible references in this paper are from The Revised Standard Version Bible: 1971 Update (Grand Rapids, MI: Zondervan Publishing House, 1971). Used by permission.

∞ The paper used in the print edition of this title meets the minimum requirements of the American National Standard for Information Services – Permanence of Paper for Printed Library Materials, ANSI Z39.48 – 1992.

C040816

Contents

Abstract 9

Acknowledgements 10

Dedication 11

Figures 12

Abbreviations 13

Introduction 15

CHAPTERS

1. Ministry Focus 21
2. State of the Art in the Project 37
3. Theoretical Foundation 59
4. Methodology 117
5. Field Experience 127
6. Reflection, Summary, and Conclusion 161

APPENDICES

A: Demographics Survey 171

B: Pre-Test Questionnaire 173

C: Post-Test Questionnaire 175

D: Confidentiality Form 179

E: Project Invitation Letter 183

F: Invitation Form Letter... 185

G: Grace and Spirit Baptism 187

Bibliography 205

Abstract

Originally a Doctor of Ministry project titled "Raising Up Biblical Eldership and Its Implications for Charismatic Ministry in the Local Church," the purpose of this study was to develop and test a template to call and disciple a group of leaders in the local church who function as elders, exercising spiritual oversight in congregational ministry, after the pattern in Numbers 11 and 1 Peter 5:1-5. A qualitative framework was chosen utilizing a comparison of a pre-test and post-test, participant journal, and recorded exit interviews. The major themes emerging from the study were: confidence in ministry, expectation in ministry, anointing in ministry, and humility. The data indicates a transformative effectiveness in ministry relative to elders being called to serve in Leadership.

Acknowledgements

I want to first thank my wife, Linda, for her constant encouragement through the entire project, including a timely prophetic word. Her love and selfless support were invaluable.

I also wish to thank Trinity Family Life Center Church in Pickerington, Ohio, for allowing me to develop the original template for Elders Ministry. It was an exciting journey in pastoral ministry. And of course, I'm thankful to the actual elders at TFLC, who were always willing to come alongside the pastor both in professional ministry and in this project for my Doctor of Ministry.

In addition, I wish to thank my D.Min. mentor, Jon Mark Ruthven, who taught us so ably in the centrality of the prophetic in the Bible. Our class discussions were so enriching; as well, several "out-of-class experiences" with Jon also helped to complete the picture for my continuing education.

Finally, a big appreciation is due to Mr. Don Swenson, Ph.D., Chairman of the Sociology Department at Mount Royal University in Calgary Alberta, Canada, for his help with the Table graphs (Figures).

Dedication

I dedicate this study to Mr. Jack Pyle, the head elder at Trinity Family Life Center Church in Pickerington, Ohio. Because of your constant encouragement and support, the elders' project has become a reality with amazing results. May you always be filled with the fullness of the measure of Christ our Lord.

Figures

Fig. 5.1: Confident in Behaviors of Salvation and Healing 139

Fig. 5.2: Confident in Deliverance and Prayer Counseling 140

Fig. 5.3: Confident in Miracles 140

Fig. 5.4: Confident in Biblical Leadership 141

Fig. 5.5: Confident in Elders Ministry Making a Real Difference 142

Fig. 5.6: Expect a Shared Responsibility in Ministry Load 145

Fig. 5.7: Confident that Regular Meetings with Elders Would Make a Difference 145

Fig. 5.8: Confident that Ongoing Training Would Make a Difference 146

Fig. 5.9: Confident in Grounding in the Word of God and Ability to Teach 149

Fig. 5.10: Spending Less than Adequate Time in Prayer 150

Fig. 5.11: Sensed Personal Support of Elders 153

Abbreviations

ANT	Anointing in Ministry
BOD	*The Book of Discipline of the United Methodist Church*
CM	Confidence in Ministry
EXP	Expectation in Ministry
HUM	Humility
TFLC	Trinity Family Life Center
UMC	United Methodist Church

Introduction

PLURALITY IN LEADERSHIP is not a foreign concept in the Bible. Moses had his seventy elders (Num. 11:16); Joshua had his elders (Josh. 7:6; 8:10); David had his elders (2 Sam. 5:3; 1 Chron. 11:3); Jesus had his disciples (Mt. 10:1); James had his elders and the Apostolic Council (Acts 15:13–22); and finally the Apostle Paul had his elders (Acts 20:17–35).[1] I suggest the contemporary church today is suffering in many respects because it has not only failed to awaken leadership empowered by the New Covenant Spirit,[2] but the church has put all her leadership hopes into one

---

[1] Unless otherwise indicated, all Bible references in this paper are from *The Revised Standard Version Bible: 1971 Update* (Grand Rapids, MI: Zondervan Publishing House, 1971).

[2] Professor Jon Ruthven has done a great service to the church in his recent book, *What's Wrong with Protestant Theology?* wherein he postulates the goal of God's interaction with man through the Bible. He states that traditional religion has avoided the intimacy that comes with direct communication with God; however, the Bible suggests that such an experience of intimacy "fulfills the promise of both the Old Covenant that is so tragically rejected (Exod. 20:18–20; Heb. 12), and the New Covenant, which seeks to place the Spirit of God directly upon us, put his prophetic words of power in our mouth (Isa. 59:21>Acts 2:39), and place his instructions (Jer. 32:33>2 Cor. 3: Heb. 8:12) or voice 'today' (Heb. 3:7, 15: 4:4, 12:25) directly into our heart.'" Jon Mark Ruthven, *What's Wrong with Protestant Theology: Tradition vs. Biblical Emphasis* (Tulsa, OK: Word & Spirit Press, 2013), 1. Is this not exactly what Paul

basket, namely the local church pastor. In the traditional church model, the pastor is trained, apprenticed, ordained, and sent out as a kind of one-man army "to equip the saints for the work of ministry" (Eph. 4:12). I believe that this model is extremely inefficient and more often than not results in pastoral burnout.[3]

This paper will argue for a replacement of the traditional approach of one man or one woman as the "point person" in the local church leadership structure to a biblically referenced eldership, as exemplified in the church of the New Testament (A.D. 50 to 100). Therefore, I have chosen a proximate design of Biblical Eldership[4] taken from the New Testament record, while arguing for a plurality of leadership, prophetically driven, charismatically gifted, and focused in a pastor/ shepherd function in the local church. The twenty-first century church cannot return to a first-century milieu, but she can and should learn from a plurality of leadership design enhanced through a prophetic template.

A Body ministry, which the New Testament clearly displays, can only serve the church as she faces a certain eschatological future. When immersing local church leadership in a prophetic grace-centered *(charis)* matrix, one stands a better chance at achieving unity and diversity in ministry, and in the process, meeting the needs of the larger Body of Christ. In this accommodation more needs are met by a greater number of people while empowered ministry becomes a mainstay of the local church.

The following template for Elders Ministry establishes a group

---

writes in Romans 8:14, 16?
[3] See *PastorBurnout.com*, accessed October 10, 2012, http://www.pastorburnout.com/.
[4] Biblical Eldership is capitalized throughout this document to indicate the biblical pattern established in the New Testament for lay leadership (elders) prior to A.D. 100.

Introduction 17

of leaders who come alongside the pastor for the purpose of spiritual oversight and congregational ministry (guidance, discernment, and stability), thereby releasing the pastor (who is frequently overwhelmed in ministry) of undue stress and fatigue in having to be the know-all, end-all in the administration of the local church in the twenty-first century. One will find disclosure for this project when analyzing the structure of the United Methodist Church (UMC).[5]

---

[5] *The Book of Discipline of the United Methodist Church* (Nashville, TN: The United Methodist Publishing House, 2008), hereafter referred to as *BOD*, delineates the parameters for pastoral ministry in the denomination. They are as follows: ¶ 340, 250–252, details the responsibilities and duties of the Elder. They begin: (A) *Related to Word and ecclesial acts*: (1) To preach the Word of God, lead in worship, read and teach the Scriptures, engage the people in study and witness: (a) to ensure faithful transmission of the Christian faith; (b) to lead people in discipleship and evangelistic outreach that others might come to know Christ and to follow him. (2) To counsel persons with personal, ethical, or spiritual struggles. (3) To perform ecclesial acts of marriage and burial: (a) to perform the marriage ceremony after due counsel with parties involved and in accordance with the laws of the state and the rules of the United Methodist Church. The decision to perform the ceremony shall be the right and responsibility of the pastor; (b) to conduct funeral and memorial services and provide care and grief counseling. (4) To visit in the homes of the church and the community, especially among the sick, aged, imprisoned, and others in need. (5) To maintain all confidences inviolate, including confessional confidences except in the cases of suspected child abuse or neglect, or in cases where mandatory reporting is required by civil law. (B) *Sacrament* : (1) To administer the sacraments of baptism and the Supper of the Lord according to Christ's ordinance: (a) to prepare the parents and sponsors before baptizing infants or children, and instruct them concerning the significance of baptism and their responsibilities for the Christian training of the baptized child; (b) to encourage reaffirmation of the baptismal covenant and renewal of baptismal vows at different stages of life; (c) to encourage people baptized in infancy or early childhood to make their profession of faith, after instruction, so that they might become professing members of the church; (d) to explain the meaning of the Lord's Supper and to encourage regular participation as a means of grace to grow in faith and

18 Biblical Eldership

The UMC, of which I am an ordained elder, is a large denomination of small churches. Seventy-five percent of the churches in the denomination have 200 members or less, with

---

holiness; (e) to select and train deacons and lay members to serve the consecrated communion elements. (2) To encourage the private and congre-gational use of the other means of grace. (C) *Order*: (1) To be the administrative officer of the local church and to assure that the organizational concerns of the congregation are adequately provided for: (a) to give pastoral support, guidance, and training to the lay leadership, equipping them to fulfill the ministry to which they are called; (b) to give oversight to the educational program of the church and encourage the use of United Methodist literature and media; (c) To be responsible for organizational faithfulness, goal setting, planning and evaluation. (d) To search out and counsel men and women for the ministry of deacons, elders, local pastors, and other church-related ministries. (2) To administer the temporal affairs of the church in their appointment, the annual conference, and the general church: (a) to administer the provisions of the Discipline [which this is only two pages of an 857-page book!]; (b) to give an account of their pastoral ministries to the charge and annual conference according to the prescribed forms; (c) to lead the congregation in the fulfillment of its mission through full and faithful payment of all apportioned ministerial support, administrative, and benevolent funds; (d) to care for all church records and local church financial obligations, and certify the accuracy of all financial, membership, and any other reports submitted by the local church to the annual conference for use in apportioning costs back to the church. (3) To participate in denominational and conference programs and training opportunities: (a) to seek out opportunities for cooperative ministries with other United Methodist pastors and churches; (b) to be willing to assume supervisory responsibilities within the connection. (4) To lead the congregation in racial and ethnic inclusiveness. (D) *Service:* (1) to embody the teachings of Jesus in servant ministries and servant leadership. (2) To give diligent pastoral leadership in ordering the life of the congregation for discipleship in the world. (3) To build the body of Christ as a caring and giving community, extending the ministry of Christ to the world. (4) To participate in community, ecumenical, and inter-religious concerns and to encourage the people to become so involved and to pray and labor for the unity of the Christian community.

sixty to eighty people in church on a given Sunday morning. The prevailing cultural model of ministry in the average local church is for the pastor to do the work of ministry while the congregation supports the pastor with a salary, a home to live in, and a minimal congregational protocol. In other words, the pastor does the ministry and the people watch and applaud.

Within this denominational model, the church continues to exhaust its pastoral gift, limit its vision and productivity, and compromise its pursuit of the Kingdom of God. The researcher's project test-drives a new model of ecclesiology[6] that is zealous for the grace (charismata) of God, while remaining passionate for human transformation. I am not necessarily arguing for a complete "overhaul" of the present denominational structure on ecclesiology, but rather a simple application to aid the pastor in the spiritual administration of the local church, whereby Biblical Eldership (plurality of leadership) would come alongside the pastor (apostolic leader) to give expression to gift-based ministry for the upbuilding and encouragement of the local body. To do this, my research uses a template of recruitment, training, mobilization, and evaluation using five churches within a 150-mile radius of United Theological Seminary. The template was given to me during my ministry years in the pastorate and successfully employed to the glory of God.

Chapter One of this dissertation discusses the synergy of my personal spiritual autobiography, my experience in pastoral ministry including the breakthrough into Elders Ministry, my ecumenical context over the years, and any personal bias or preconceived beliefs about the project.

Chapter Two delineates conflicting views of the Ministry of Elders from two basic theological positions. I take issue with the two positions while suggesting that the present model

---

[6] Ecclesiology is "the science of church organization and management." *Webster's New Universal Unabridged Dictionary*, 2nd ed., s.v. "ecclesiology."

summarized in this paper may present a median outcome when actually practiced in the field. A literature review with analysis is included.

Chapter Three develops the biblical, historical, and theological foundations for the ministry of elders. It traces the history of elders prior to A.D. 100 as well as supportive evidence throughout the history of the church. Theological positions that support Elders Ministry are analyzed relative to the present project. Conclusions are drawn on the basis of the evidence.

Chapter Four identifies the methodology utilized in the study. This will include an explanation of why the research design was chosen as well as triangulation of methods for data gathering. This chapter establishes the hypothesis, the measurement parameters, and the instrumentation used in the project.

Chapter Five recounts the field experience. The chapter includes the analytical process I used, an explanation of the demographics of the participants, which establishes a well-rounded sample, an analysis of the data and findings, and a summary of the outcomes.

Chapter Six includes my reflections, summations, and conclusion. Concluding remarks will include how the project could be improved and will give suggestions for implementation of the template on a larger-scale basis. I compare the projected measurement of the project with the actual outcome and, lastly, recommend topics for future research.

1

Ministry Focus

GROWING UP IN DAYTON, OHIO, in the late 1950's was a wonderful experience. I was raised in a middle-class home with many neighbors who were thoughtful and caring people. Ours was a well-established nuclear family with a loving and caring mother and father and one sister, who was the firstborn. My father managed a dairy called Blossom Hill Dairy, "the dairy with Real Cows." My grandfather owned the dairy, which was located on West Third Street in Dayton. Our home environment was stable with no recollection of marital dissonance. My experience was secure, solid, and wonderful.

Out of all the girls I dated in high school, there was only one "crown jewel": Linda Cremeens, whose last name is now Kelso. Following high school graduation, I decided to attend Ohio State University, and Linda went off to Bowling Green State University. We continued to date and see each other on infrequent weekends. After a year at college, we decided to get married, so Linda dropped out of college and came back to Dayton to work and save money for our marriage.

Following a slow and distracted start, I began to focus on college and grades, getting As and Bs throughout the remainder of college. It's amazing what one can do when one gets focused, even if being average in learning. We married on June 7, 1969, while I was beginning my senior year at Ohio State. In September of that year, we drove to New Jersey to visit my sister and brother-in-law. On the way we stopped in Carlisle, Pennsylvania, because Linda had developed a medical condition, requiring a brief visit to the hospital. Following the trip for medical treatment we returned to our hotel for the evening. Simply turning on the TV that evening changed our lives because Billy Graham was preaching a crusade and God Almighty had our number.

I had always been fascinated by this evangelist, even in high school. His gaze was almost hypnotic as he preached the gospel. As we sat on the side of the bed and ate, I felt my heart being pulled right into the television. As John Wesley said the night he was converted, May 24, 1738, "I felt my heart strangely warmed." When Dr. Graham gave the altar call, we both knelt by the bed and dedicated our lives to Christ.

I had really been changed from the inside out by the power of the Holy Spirit: I had been truly "born again." I remember trying to explain to my sister and brother-in-law what had happened in our lives. They thought we were in some kind of a religious cult. However, a few years later, they too received Christ and began attending a Baptist church. In fact, we saw our entire family dedicate themselves to God in a fresh way during the following years.

As a postscript, we returned to the hospital on our way home only to find that there was no record or our being there just a few days earlier. My wife had taken only one dose of the medicine and was completely healed. Hindsight informed us that this entire episode was a divine appointment to galvanize our lives for God.

During my senior year of college, a definite "call to ministry" developed in our lives. Interestingly enough, I literally graduated from college one day and began seminary the next. The first day at United Theological Seminary, I met a fellow pastor from the Western Pennsylvania Conference who became a very close friend. Early in the fall of 1970, he took me to an interdenominational charismatic prayer meeting held at the Convent of the Precious Blood on Salem Avenue in Dayton. Upon entering the meeting, we observed Methodists, Presbyterians, Catholics, and Baptists all worshipping the Lord together with hands raised and smiles on their faces. I did not remember people singing with smiles on their faces at my home church. At intervals, they would all speak in tongues, and prophetic words would come forth. It didn't take long to realize God was all over the meeting. I realized they had experienced something called the Baptism in the Holy Spirit. I also knew that this experience was destined for my life as well. A few weeks later, I was baptized in the Holy Spirit and spoke in tongues. The experience was a real spiritual shot of adrenaline, and it has never ceased. I can truly say it was one of the great galvanizing moments of my entire life.

Ministry Context at Trinity United Methodist

Following seminary, I was appointed to a small country church in Pickerington, Ohio: Trinity United Methodist. The congregation was formed in the year 1866 under the Evangelical Association with Jacob Albright as Bishop. Albright was a Wesleyan, groomed to take the Methodist movement to the German people. The Evangelical Association merged with the United Brethren Church in 1964, which in turn merged with the Methodist church in 1968 at the General Conference in Dallas, Texas. We are now the UMC.

From its inception, Trinity had remained a very small fellowship, with another church on the same charge until early in

1973. At that time Trinity decided to grow and employ a full-time pastor. I preached my first sermon on Father's Day 1973. From the years 1973 to 1978, Trinity realized consistent growth. In 1978 the church experienced a real awakening in almost every area of the church life. This was due in part to the consistent, uncompromising preaching of the Bible as God's truth for His people. A real vision for ministry to the community was born in the hearts of the people. Trinity was becoming a congregation that desperately desired to see people reconciled to God through Jesus Christ. In all the services, an opportunity for reconciliation and commitment to Christ was extended to those in attendance.

How does one summarize being the pastor of the same church for thirty-eight years? I will attempt to paint the picture in broad strokes. From 1973 to 1983, the church grew from sixty in worship to over 500. We had gone through a major building program in 1981 with two morning worship services and an evening service every week. I was drowning in success. However, the workload became almost oppressive. The church did not have paid staff. Only part-time volunteer help enabled the church to run successfully.

At this juncture, I knew something needed to give. So I sought the Lord, and the Lord took me to Numbers 11. There Moses found himself in a similar position when God said:

> Gather for me seventy men of the elders of Israel, whom you know to be the elders of the people of Israel, and officers over them; and bring them to the tent of meeting, and let them take their stand there with you. And I will come down and talk with you there; and I will take some of the spirit which is upon you and put it upon them; and they shall bear the burden of the people with you, that you may not bear it yourself alone. (Numbers 11:16–17)

Then God anoints them for supernatural ministry:

> So Moses went out and told the people the words of the Lord; and he gathered seventy men of the elders of the people, and placed them round about the tent. Then the Lord came down in the cloud and spoke to him, and took some of the spirit that was upon him and put it upon the seventy elders; and when the spirit rested upon them, they prophesied. But they did so no more. (Numbers 11:24-25)

After reading and praying, I followed the same instruction that was given to Moses. This turned out to be the single most important decision I made in thirty-eight years of ministry, and it set me on a path leading to the present dissertation project.

Continuing on, from 1983 to 1993 the church purchased thirty acres of land across the road in anticipation of future growth. With thirty acres of land, the possibilities were great indeed, well into the future. As one member said as we considered buying the land, "You better get as much as you can; they are not making any more of it." Just two years later in 1995, the church did relocate across the road on the new land, built a new facility, and struck oil to boot. The well pump is still producing oil revenue, free of charge!

In addition, during these years, we raised three wonderful children and all that goes with it. These three have since produced seven grandchildren who are the light in our day. I was blessed to take a traditional evangelical country church and turn it into a full-blown large suburban charismatic church. The church's story traveled through our annual conference and across the nation through our national Aldersgate Renewal Fellowship (a charismatic enclave of Spirit-filled United Methodist believers from across the nation). I was called upon to teach at our national events, giving hope to many others in the denomination who were hungry for a move of God across the church.

Many leaders who have encountered the ministry at Trinity

United Methodist have described it as a "bridge church." As the designation implies, we were known to bridge the gap between the traditional denominational church experience and the independent charismatic Word churches that were springing up all over the country. We found that many people appreciated the stability of a denominational church without the stifling effect of a traditional ecclesiology. This provided for flexible worship experiences where a life-giving flow of the Holy Spirit could minister to the people assembled. We reached a kind of balance in our worship services that equipped us to be able to minister to many different kinds of Christian expressions without disrupting the flow of what God wanted to do during the service.

Since Trinity was the first charismatic church in our district, one of the basic callings as a congregation was to minister to other local churches and to receive those whom God would send. In this sense, we became a "refreshing" or "filling station" for many tired and worn-out denominational persons (including clergy) who were in need of restoration and growth. We realized that we were called to minister to the UMC at large, sharing what we had learned with all who were interested and hungry for a new walk with God. We did not plan this journey; it just happened as we tried to be obedient to the leading of the Holy Spirit through our course in ministry.

Context

Presently I am in a transition period, launching an apostolic, traveling preaching and teaching ministry to our nation and to the nations. I have traveled to many parts of the world while still being a full-time pastor, and now the invitations seem to be increasing. I have asked myself many times, "Why has this all happened to me?" For the purposes of this study, the answer is twofold.

First, in 1984 I held a special preaching mission at Trinity

Church with an evangelist named Davy Jo Hissom (now deceased), who to this day has remained the most powerful evangelist/pastor I have ever known. From Charleston, West Virginia, Davy was a bit raw but carried an unusual anointing. He left a profound effect on my life. One evening during revival services Davy called out the author with the following prophetic word:

> The Holy Ghost has been showing me something with your pastor. God is going to open some doors in the near future for him to go out from here. And listen to me, Body, he won't be out on the road full-time; he is your pastor. God wants you to share this man with the world. God's got a work in him to take to the Methodist Church. It's there. They wouldn't receive a guy like me, but they will Scott. God says you're the body, he's the mouthpiece, but you are the body and if you'll share him, God's going to bless this church in abundance. It's no accident Pastor Bob came; it's no accident God's done the things He's done.
>
> For I will say indeed this night my son, I've raised you up and you'll not just pastor, you'll be an apostle, saith God. And you'll go to other churches and those things which I teach you here, you'll impart to those shepherds, and they'll begin to flow just like this. Oh yes, for have you not known that many of God have picked up the mantles from here and there and even that's in your deepest secrets; you said, 'God, what kind of man was John Wesley?' God said the same kind of man I am going to make of you. And some would say oh, he's such a small man. God said know you this night and never, ever forget it; your inner man is a giant, he is a giant, saith God. (May 16, 1984)

Within a week of that word, my telephone began to ring with invitations to go out and speak in other churches. I had not previously conducted any special meetings for other pastors prior to this word, although it had been in my heart to take my message of spirit-filled Christianity on the road. The following years I preached all over Ohio, all across the nation, and even around the world. It was really amazing.

The second reason for understanding a broader venue in my speaking journeys is tied to John Wesley, which Davy mentioned in his prophetic word. The answer comes from Wesley's journal dated June 11, 1739. Wesley had received a request from his friends in London at Fetter-Lane (a Moravian outpost for discipleship) "to come thither as soon as possible, our brethren in Fetter-Lane being in great confusion for want of my presence and advice."[7] In Wesley's response to these brethren, he makes the following statement: "I look upon all the world as my parish; therefore I mean, that in whatever part of it I am, I judge it meet, right, and my bounden duty, to declare unto all that are willing to hear, the glad tidings of salvation."[8]

In reflecting on Wesley's statement "the world is my parish," I feel drawn to a similar track in ministry. Perhaps it is part of our DNA as Methodist preachers. Francis Asbury was sent to America in 1771 by John Wesley to evangelize the nation for Christ. John Wigger says, "In 1775 fewer than one out of every eight hundred Americans was a Methodist; by 1812, Methodists numbered one out of every thirty-five Americans."[9] My point here is not to push denominationalism, but to lift up prophetic evangelism as directed by the Holy Spirit. I believe God has placed me in such a venue for evangelism and given me a platform to travel and minister in the anointing so that people can firmly be set free in the power of Jesus Christ. As Wesley said, "God in scripture commands me to instruct the ignorant, reform the wicked, and confirm the virtuous."[10] I believe this is what I am to do in the remainder of my days.

---

[7] John Wesley, *The Works of John Wesley*, 3rd. ed. (Grand Rapids, MI: Baker Book House, 1978), 1:199.
[8] Wesley, *Works*, 1:201.
[9] John Wigger, *American Saint: Francis Asbury & the Methodists* (New York: Oxford University Press, 2009), 10.
[10] Wesley, *Journal*, June 11, 1739, *Works*, 1:201.

In working broadly with pastors over the last thirty years, one of the problem areas I have encountered in ministry is that of clergy discouragement and the feeling that the pastor's job is inevitably a "go it alone" experience. I regularly receive calls from frustrated pastors across the nation, seeking counsel on a problem in their church or a personal struggle they are experiencing in ministry. Having experienced many of these issues, periodically our church would host events for clergy, knowing they would come to a fully charismatic church and receive a "safe zone" atmosphere as well as some real-time practical help.

The Christian pastor is a uniquely isolated animal, a kind of enigma. Pastors live their lives in a fishbowl under unrelenting observation from others while at the same time finding little time or space to be alone. In addition, the pastors' time is not their own, even though they are for the most part their own boss. Their schedules are driven by unexpected events, regularly scheduled meetings, and weekly deadlines. Again, I have worked extensively over the course of the ministry, and the picture is not pretty. Invariably, when I have gone out to speak in another church, I know that a good part of the ministry time during the trip will be to the pastor and the spouse. In many cases this was the most significant impact of my ministry during traveling across the nation.

Pastors are usually always open to my counsel while on ministry trips because: a) they invited me; b) they need some help and encouragement from someone who has walked the walk; and c) the counsel is private and safe, where they can truly open up without fear that their innermost frustrations will wind up as conversation on the front stoop of the church. All this becomes vitally important if the pastor is going to lead the church in renewal. He or she must first experience renewal themselves, spiritually, mentally, emotionally, and physically.

On a site previously noted entitled PastorBurnout.com, Daniel Sherman lists statistics and resources for pastors experiencing discouragement, exhaustion, and burnout in ministry. Quoting from a *New York Times* article, Sherman adds: "Members of the clergy now suffer from obesity, hypertension and depression at rates higher than most Americans. In the last decade, their use of antidepressants has risen, while their life expectancy has fallen. Many would change jobs if they could."[11] The following are a few of his stats leading to the condition of burnout:

- Administrative Burnout: too much time spent in low-reward activities such as correspondence, bulletins, newsletters, website browsing, purchasing church supplies, doing janitorial functions, attending endless meetings, and so on.

- Family Concerns: marital strife within the pastor's family due to unrealistic expectations, inadequate finances, and minimal time spent with spouse, pressure to have the perfect family while spending all your time away from the home on pastoral ministry, and so on.

- Financial Pressure: stress around inadequate salaries, pressure to watch what you spend, driving inadequately maintained vehicles, feeling you have to always use coupons and search out every sale, and so on.

- Conflict Issues: the pastor is constantly putting out fires and dealing with petty conflicts; someone is always unhappy; people are stuck in their comfort zones.

- Sin Disruption: indulging in distractions to ease the pain such as food, television, secret fantasies, pornography, affairs, and unconfessed sin.

---

[11] Quoted in Daniel Sherman, "Burnout Statistics," *PastorBurnout.com*, accessed October 10, 2012, http://www.pastorburnout.com/pastor-burnout-statistics.html.

- Psychological Pressures: too many people demanding the pastor's time, people wanting counsel or advice but rarely following through on the advice, feelings of being ill-prepared to "solve" others' problems, the difficulty of balancing leadership and servanthood, and so forth.

- Theological Causes: having to explain life situations and tragedies such as premature death, earthquakes, disease, terrorism, traffic accidents and others; constantly seeing the worst of humanity while teaching others to strive for the best of humanity.[12]

The above list could be expanded many times over including such things as health problems, scheduling problems, not enough hours in the day, not enough time with God and lack of adequate time for prayer, the fact that everyone in the church is your boss, and many more. It is no wonder that only 10 percent of all pastors who begin in ministry at an early age make it to active retirement in their sixties. Mr. Sherman is a former burnt-out pastor and has researched this subject over many years. His statistics section does not bode well for the future of ministry, either. Consider these:

- The average length of a pastorate today is four years.
- The median salary of clergy today lands at $32,000.
- 53 percent of pastors believe the church is showing little positive impact on the society around them.
- 60 percent of pastors believe that church ministry has negatively impacted their passion for church work.
- 80 percent of pastors have bachelor's degrees and half of them have master's degrees, and yet they remain among the lowest-paid professionals in society.[13]

---

[12] Sherman, "Burnout Statistics."
[13] Sherman, "Burnout Statistics."

When considering these and other statistics concerning pastoral ministry in America, it is not difficult to see how the average pastor's life can go south very fast. We human beings simply are not wired to negotiate this many negatives on a regular basis while at the same time expected to be on top of the world ourselves. It is absolutely unrealistic.

As I would encounter discouraged pastors along the way, I found myself sharing a very helpful template that I received from a one-day pastor's seminar in basic youth conflicts with Bill Gothard as the instructor. The following template has proven very useful over the years, not only in my own life, but in the lives of other pastors to whom I have ministered in the field.[14]

It seems that discouragement is one of Satan's most effective weapons. One definition is "to decrease courage; to be fainthearted; to lose hope; to be dismayed." The stages of discouragement can range from mild to strong to disabling. A basic cause could be attributed to putting down the shield of faith (Ephesians 6:16). At its base is a lie from Satan, which can manifest in fiery darts of fear, unbelief, bitterness, or self-pity. Some apparent reasons can be found in Numbers 21:4, the hardness of the way; Nehemiah 4:10, the difficulty of the task; Psalm 73:2-3, the prosperity of the wicked; and Proverbs 13:12, a delay in the fulfillment of desires. One may ask, how does one conquer discouragement? Perhaps the following bullet points may prove instructive:

- Remove any guilt by repentance and confessions (1 Timothy 1:18-19). A good conscience is neither too broad nor too narrow, a good conscience is consistent, and a good conscience is forgiving.

---

[14] Bill Gothard, "Dealing with Discouragement," Institute in Basic Youth Conflicts, Senior Pastor's Seminar, September 17, 1981, Dayton, OH.

- Above, all take the shield of faith and quench the fiery darts of the enemy (Ephesians 6:16). Identify counterfeits by knowing the real thing (getting to know the truth and being able to recognize it); identify and cast down Satan's lies (2 Corinthians 10:5).

- Encourage your heart in the Lord (1 Samuel 30:6). God lays down some methods whereby we can level the playing field. Here we see that David draws strength in a situation beyond his control. He is encouraged by past mercies performed by God in his life. With this we need to meditate on scriptural promises, especially before bed, and to always read, mark, learn, and inwardly digest.

- Remove yourself from fearful people (Deuteronomy 20:8–9).

- Surround yourself with wise, courageous, encouraging people. When Paul writes of comforting others (2 Corinthians 1:4), "comfort" expresses the sense of "making people strong, able to stand."

- Avoid major decisions (Galatians 6:9).

- Overcome the pride of not telling your spiritual superiors or best friends that you are discouraged and need their prayers (James 5:16).

- Focus on your position in Christ and consider what He endured (Hebrews 12:1; Romans 8:1).

- Discuss how God can use this for good (Romans 8:29). There is a silver lining in every cloud. Someone said that a lame man came to join the Greek army, but the other soldiers laughed at him and said, "How can you run with that lame leg?" The lame man replied, "I came to fight, not to run."[15]

---

[15] Gothard, "Dealing with Discouragement."

Conclusion

The above-discussed challenges lead me to address a long-term problem that traditionally employs only short-term solutions. Common therapy approaches to the pastor burnout problem are usually such things as time away from the job to reflect and renew; sabbatical study and rest; conferences and seminars that address the issue; performance reviews with an eye to redistribute some pastoral responsibilities; medical therapies, including drug therapy; and a host of others. Many of these in and of themselves are not necessarily wrong. The problem is, in most cases, they are a temporary fix at best. The same problems and challenges in ministry that caused the burnout in the first place have not gone away.

I believe an insertion of an Elders Ministry template in the local church will enhance the spiritual administration of the church and bring needed help to the pastor through the supernatural gifts of the Holy Spirit working in an elder's discipling model. I realize that I cannot invade many of these pastoral situations like a knight in shining armor and "rescue" them from their present plight in ministry. However, for pastors who are frustrated and feel stuck in ministry, perhaps the present model of Elders Ministry will be just the thing to move them off dead center and spark a different sprit in the congregation. Most congregations will receive a dedicated group of servant leaders who love the people and have their best interest at heart, and will respond positively to their contribution.

Therefore, my grounded theory framework has produced data to suggest a template for Elders Ministry that is open to the prophetic invasion of the Holy Spirit coupled with the development of elders in the local church. It may have a dramatic positive effect not only on the quality of Christian ministry but also on the effectiveness and longevity of the present crisis in attrition among Christian pastors in the twenty-first century.

From these reflections and my own ministry experience of thirty-eight years, this project carries the potential to bless and encourage pastoral ministry in the UMC and perhaps help insulate the church from the grip of further denominational decline. Far too many pastors have become resigned to a mediocre ministry format, and far too many churches have become comfortable with a mentality of a religious social club, where new members are welcomed only on the basis of denominational affiliation wed to casual commitment. The church of Jesus Christ can and must do better than that.

The New Testament says that Jesus is coming back for a church "without spot or wrinkle" (Eph. 5:27). I am not sure what all that means, but I am confident that it does not mean a church that has resigned itself to a "business as usual" format. When a group of disciples tap into all that is available to them in God, it will ruin them for the ordinary. I invite the reader to come along, and let's get ruined together.

2

State of the Art in the Project

Conjunction of Theoretical and Practical

THIS BOOK ARISES OUT of a single text in the Old Testament in which a breakthrough in proportional ministry propelled me on a catalytic journey, beginning in the year 1984. Ten years into a successful appointment in the UMC, Trinity UMC in Pickerington, Ohio, grew from sixty people in morning worship to over 500, encompassing two morning services and an evening service. In the interim, the workload increased beyond my capacity to adequately meet. I cried out to the Lord for direction. In short order, God revealed His Word in Numbers 11. Therein, finding Moses in a similar predicament, the words seemed to jump off the page as God's revelation flooded my heart:

> And the Lord said to Moses, "Gather for me seventy men of the elders of Israel, whom you know to be the elders of the people and officers over them; and bring them to the tent of meeting, and let them take their stand there with you. And I will come

> down and talk with you there; and I will take some of the spirit which is upon you and put it upon them; and they shall bear the burden of the people with you that you may not bear it yourself alone." (Num. 11:16-17)
>
> So Moses went out and told the people the words of the Lord; and he gathered seventy men of the elders of the people, and placed them around about the tent. Then the Lord came down in the cloud and spoke to him, and took some of the spirit that was upon him and put it upon the seventy elders; and when the spirit rested upon them, they prophesied. But they did so not more. (Num. 11:24-25)

In my opinion, the above pericope from Numbers seemed to be the exact remedy for an overworked local pastor. Immediately the ministry of Biblical Eldership commenced at Trinity Church. Pastor Rick Warren asks the question in the most widely sold Christian book in modern times: "What do the words committees, elections, majority rule, boards, board members, parliamentary procedures, voting and vote have in common? None of these words are found in the New Testament."[16] Typically the American pastor has attempted to superimpose an American form of government on the church in an attempt to manage workload and personal fatigue. Usually what ensues is a kind of church bureaucracy, slowing down the decision-making process and preventing the kind of growth experienced in the New Testament book of Acts.

In contrast, I suggest in this book that the fastest and most efficient method to stimulate effective ministry in the local church is to employ an Elders Ministry as seen in the New Testament. Biblical revelation in both the Old and New Testaments and my

---

[16] Rick Warren, *The Purpose Driven Church: Growth without Compromising Your Message & Mission* (Grand Rapids, MI; Zondervan Publishing House, 1995), 377.

own experience in the field have proven that calling and discipling a group of leaders for local church eldership, wherein they come alongside the pastor to help guard and guide the sheep, becomes an efficient ecclesiological structure. The heart of New Testament ministry is to employ the gifts of the Spirit through mobilizing the larger Body of Christ (1 Cor. 12:11).

When we read the New Testament, we find that Jesus was not jealous or possessive (guarded) when it came to His use of God's power as a demonstration of His Kingdom. In fact He told His disciples, "Truly, truly I say unto you he who believes in me will also do the works that I do; and greater works than these will he do, because I go to the Father" (John 14:12). What were those works but healings, deliverances, raising the dead, and all manifestations of the collision of light with darkness? (Matt. 11:12). By this we see God's Kingdom breaking into the spiritual darkness of the present fallen world.[17]

Jesus knew that man was flawed and prone to error and mistake, and yet this did not discourage Him from trusting His Kingdom into their hands. In the process, He also knew that the Holy Spirit was coming. Too many pastors avoid carrying the "power of Jesus" into the world because of a misguided notion of making the gospel irrelevant, which usually means making it culturally palatable. In foreign missions this is referred to as contextualization. Domestically, it usually translates into "dumbing down" the gospel so as to not offend "seeker" available candidates. However, in the wake of this "contextualization," a sort of toothless Christianity emerges that

---

[17] And we see this is exactly what those who followed Jesus did in the work of His influence on their lives. This can be seen in a series of summary statements concerning their ministry fruit. See: 1 Cor. 4:20; 1 Peter 4:6; Heb. 2:3-4; Gal. 3:5; Rom. 15:19; 1 Cor. 2:4-5; Eph. 1:19-20; 1 Thess. 1:5; Acts 15:19.

is inept at producing full-blown disciples whose lives are characterized by those we see who followed Moses and Jesus, some of whom were elders and all of whom were disciples.

I believe I am called to help pastors and churches navigate through the often confusing maze of options and programs, many of which are good, yet not quite good enough. God has a will and purpose for each local church, and the pastor is called to help the people discern what that will is and how to release it in the local context. A plurality of leadership as seen in the New Testament documents will help to put the church and the pastor on sure footing through a shared leadership design.

Literature Review

Most churches and denominations employ some form of elder ministry in the administration of their ecclesiastical protocol,[18] and yet very few do it with a simple New Testament design operating in the power of the Holy Spirit for oversight and ministry. The Old Testament baseline for the present model under research as stated earlier comes from Numbers 11:16–19. The model was confirmed in Isaiah's experience and noted in Isaiah 63:11c, 12a, and 14, as well as David's journey noted in Ps. 105:5,

---

[18] "The Protestant Reformation represented a major revolt against the authority claims of the clerical hierarchy of the Roman Catholic Church. Reformers denied the superior authority of the pope and redefined the nature and function of clergy. This taught that clergy were to be ministers of the Word, not 'priests' who mediated the sacraments to a subservient laity." As a result, "what started as an attempt to reform the corrupt and often abusive Catholic clergy, set in motion changes in the authority structure of church and society. The variations in church organizational structures which emerged within Protestantism are all derivatives of Episcopal, Presbyterian, or Congregational models." B. Gunther and D. Heidebrecht, "The Elusive Biblical Model of Leadership," *Direction* 28, no. 2 (1999): 157.

27; Ps. 106:22; and Ps. 107:20. The cry of Moses to Yahweh in Numbers 11 set in motion a prophetic model of Biblical Eldership that carried through into the New Testament and beyond. "In ancient Israel, the term 'elder' was an imprecise way of referring to those who were recognized as the wise and mature leaders in the community because their authority and power were based on existing family/community relationships. These were people to whom respect was instinctively given because of their age and experience."[19] Rod Parrott puts it this way: "Elders is the middle term in the sequence, old—older—oldest. Its primary denotation is relative chronological age."[20]

Professor Roger D. Cotton of the Assemblies of God Theological Seminary in Springfield, MO, believes that the events in Numbers 11 are intended "as a paradigm/prototype of what should be expected for all God-ordained leadership."[21] The passage displays an obvious interconnectedness between the Spirit of God and the leadership of God's people through the prophetic.[22] In some sense, because of Moses's plea, "Would that all the Lord's people were prophets, that the Lord would put his Spirit upon them" (Num. 11:29), our lives even into the twenty-first century have been affected. The reason is that this particular plea under the inspiration of the Holy Spirit foreshadowed both God's intention for His people, voiced in the prophet Joel 2:1-4 and realized at Pentecost (Acts 2:1-4, 16-21). As Professor Cotton says, "A divinely initiated, prophetic-speech event in both passages was clearly presented as evidence to the observers that

---

[19] Gunther and Heidebrecht, "Elusive," 154. Also, see R. Alastair Campbell, *The Elders* (Edinburgh, Scotland: T&T Clark, 1994), 239.
[20] Rod Parrott, "New Testament Elders in Their Context," *Impact* 4, no. 1 (1980): 28.
[21] Roger D. Cotton, "The Pentecostal Significance of Numbers 11," *Journal of Pentecostal Theology*, 10, no. 1 (2001): 7.
[22] Cotton, "Pentecostal Significance," 3.

the Spirit was working in those chosen for ministry function."[23] Furthermore, Dr. Jon Ruthven makes a strong case that this prophetic anointing was also foreshadowed by the prophet Isaiah in 59:20–21 and fulfilled in Acts 2:39, confirming a major covenant promise for all of God's people.[24]

Reflecting on the above verses, Professor Timothy L. Ashley remarks, "Perhaps the experience of the shared Spirit is even the antidote for the weary, harried, threatened leader."[25] "It is also important to expect that divine provision will often come through other people empowered by his Spirit."[26] All this suggests that in some sense early on in the biblical story, a plurality of leadership was both requested and supplied through divine means with respect to the governing of God's people. The signal action of this request became a supernatural prophetic anointing, validating in the eyes of the community gathered, that those who were called were also commissioned.

Furthermore, when Moses experienced the validating action of the Spirit of God transferred from him to seventy elders, the effect was so dramatic that he spontaneously uttered: "Would that all the Lord's people were prophets, that the Lord would put his Spirit upon them" (Num. 11:29). This "ministry under the anointing" became a vital resource in leading God's people, and in some measure extends even to us in the present day. It is this anointing that the present study is arguing for as vital in the administration of God's people in the local church. For too long we have attempted man-initiated resources to accomplish God-

---

[23] Cotton, "Pentecostal Significance," 8. See also Roger Stronstad, *The Charismatic Theology of St. Luke* (Peabody, MA: Hendrickson Publishing Co., 1984), 22.
[24] Ruthven, *What's Wrong*, 1.
[25] Timothy R. Ashley, *The Book of Numbers: NICOT* (Grand Rapids, MI: Wm. B. Eerdmans Publishing Co., 1993), 217.
[26] Cotton, "Pentecostal Significance," 10.

initiated mandates. The time for the shift to anointed ministry, prophetically driven, charismatically gifted, with its locus in the pastoral/shepherd function, is upon us if the traditional denominational church is to survive.

Since this project will advocate for a return to Biblical Eldership, it will be important to grasp from the outset a composite sense of New Testament teaching on the subject. To begin with, an overwhelming majority of scholarship argues that the terms "elder" (*presbyteroi*) and "bishop" (*episkopoi*) were used interchangeably in the New Testament documents. Surely church historians have recorded how these terms have changed in emphasis and location through the centuries, but in the New Testament period, they were seen as complimentary to one another. Respected scholar Raymond Brown reminds us, "The interchangeability of *presbyteros* and *episkopos* is seen not only in the Pastorals (Titus 1:5-7; 1 Tim. 3:1; 5:17) but also in Acts 28, where those who have previously been designated as the *presbyteroi* of the church of Ephesus are told: 'Take heed to yourselves and to all the flock in which the Holy Spirit has made you *episkopoi* to shepherd the church of God.'"[27] Additionally, Guenther and Heidebrecht remind us that "the writers of the New Testament use these terms interchangeably for leaders of the church."[28] The three terms for church leaders found in this

---

[27] Raymond E. Brown, "*Episkope* and *Episkopos*: The New Testament Evidence," *Interface*, 2, no. 1 (1979): 337. Dr. Brown goes on to say, "Similarly, in 1 Peter 5:2-3, Peter addresses himself to the *presbyteroi,* 'Feed the flock, being supervisors (*episkopountes*) not by coercion but willingly.'"

[28] Guenther and Heidebrecht, "Elusive," 155. "Initially leadership was grounded in the Apostles themselves and believers were directed by their teaching (Acts 2:42). A division of leadership function was deemed necessary when care for the poor became too much for this small group of leaders (Acts 6:1-4). Deacons were appointed while the Apostles devoted themselves to prayer and the teachings of God's word.

passage (Acts 20:17-28) — elder, overseer, and shepherd — arise as the language of basic leadership in the New Testament churches. "*Elders* provided wisdom and maturity, *overseers* watched over, and *shepherds* fed, guided, and protected the church."[29]

As we look more carefully at the kind of character traits required for this level of church oversight, we find the following ones rise to the top: maturity, character, humility, ability to teach, circumspectness (watching over one's self), shepherding (guard, guide, protect), commitment to headship (1 Peter 5:14), and the ability to mimic Christ's relationship to His church, which Professor Dale Coulter, Associate Professor of Historical Theology, School of Divinity, Regent University, has termed "vocational identity."[30] The above characteristics are intermingled

---

Eventually the Apostles' ministry took them beyond the church in Jerusalem which necessitated further changes in church leadership structure. A passing reference to the *elders* in Jerusalem in Acts 11:30 suggest that the terminology of elders, familiar to Jewish Christianity, had been carried over from the synagogue to the New Testament church." Continuing, the authors say, "As the church spread beyond Israel, the Gentile congregations started by Paul arose within extended households and met together in homes. The elders of the homes or family were naturally recognized as the leaders of the newly formed churches. These elders continued their role of overseeing, protecting, and caring for these 'families' of believers. Near the end of Paul's missionary journeys while on his way back to Jerusalem, he sent to Ephesus for the elders of the church to meet him (Acts 20:17). He pleads with them to 'guard yourselves and all the flock of God of which the Holy Spirit has made you overseers to shepherd the church of God.'" (Acts 20:28), p. 154-155.

[29] Guenther and Heidebrecht, "Elusive," 155.

[30] Dale M. Coulter, "Christ, the Spirit, and Vocation: Initial Reflections on a Pentecostal Ecclesiology," *Pro Ecclesia* 19, no. 3 (2010): 319. Coulter says: "To talk of Jesus in this way (vocational identity) is to identify the Spirit's activity in the actualization of his twin vocation to be the new human being (*modus vivendi*) and to call others to embrace this new humanity through the proclamation of the kingdom of God (*mission*

in the New Testament co-terms of presbyter (*presbyteroi*), bishop (*episkopoi*), and shepherd (*poimonete*).³¹ This helps to explain why "a late second century congregation would elect a supervisor (*episkopos,* bishop), a council of elders or presbyters, and a supporting staff of servants or deacons."³²

In this early church amalgamation of leadership, the members of the churches also had a responsibility to make it work in a way that brings honor to Jesus and advances His Kingdom. J. W. Roberts reminds us of some of these essential characteristics.³³

---

dei)." In other words the church, which is activated by the same spirit that led Jesus (Romans 8:11), will both internalize and display the character of Jesus to the world and with the same fruit.

³¹ Guenther and Heidebrecht, "Elusive," 155. Indeed, they go on to give an excellent summary of these co-terms: "The qualifications for an overseer in Paul's letter to Timothy include the ability to teach (1 Tim. 3:1-2). Later in the same letter Paul refers to how the church should treat its elders (5:17, 19). Similarly, after Paul tells Titus to 'appoint elders in ever town' (1:5), he then describes the characteristics of an overseer (1:7). Peter's instruction for elders is to 'shepherd the flock' willingly and eagerly without domineering those for whom they are responsible (1 Peter 5:1-3). In the NT church elders oversee and shepherd, overseers are identified as the elders, and shepherds as well as overseers should be able to teach (feed) believers. Leaders are identified and chosen on the basis of their maturity, character, and giftedness. Elders were those affirmed as mature and growing (Eph. 4:13). The concern for an overseer's character (1 Tim. 3:1-7) acknowledges that for one to oversee others one needed to be watching over oneself. The ability to shepherd, coupled with the ability to teach, was recognized as a gift distributed by God's Spirit as he determines" (p. 155).

³² Paul Rorem, "Mission and Ministry in the Early Church; Bishop, Presbyters and Deacons," *Currents in Theology and Mission* 17, no. 1 (1990): 18.

³³ J. W. Roberts, "Eldership: The Rulership of Elders," *Firm Foundation* (March 25, 1958). "The duty of members toward the elders includes 'knowing them' (1 Thess. 5:12), 'honoring them' (1 Tim. 5:17), 'obeying them' (*peithesthe*) (Heb. 13:17), and 'yielding' or 'giving way to' (*hupeikete*) them (Heb. 13:17). The word here translated [as] 'obey'

Collectively, this all paints a picture of New Testament leadership, the spirit of which we would be wise to recover. The implementation phase of this project will do all in its power to capture the true spirit of the New Testament leadership laid down for us by the Apostles and senior leaders of the first-century church.

The Influence of Charisma in the Early Church Leaders

Of the early church leaders who had an influence in directing the unfolding of the church even into the Gentile world, the name of James, the brother of Jesus, comes to the fore. In Galatians 1:19, Paul commends James among the Apostles and in Galatians 2: 9, James is mentioned as a pillar in the early church. Dale Coulter reminds us that "historically speaking, the mother church of early Christianity was the Jerusalem church."[34] And Luke places James as the head of this church. "It is James who presides over the first council of the church in order to decide the precise manner in which the Gentiles form part of the one people of God even

---

(*peitho*) means to 'be persuaded by,' 'to be convinced by,' 'to take the advice of.' Compare its use in Acts 5:39 (the council takes Gamaliel's advice); Acts 18:4; 23:21, 27:11; Gal. 5:7; James 3:3). All these words (as Farrar in the *Cambridge Greek Testament* on Heb. 13:17 points out) *as expressions of the exercise of power* are vague and ambiguous. They do not indicate any kind of naked 'authority' or 'power' on the part of the bishop or 'obedience' in the real sense on the part of the saints'" (p. 55). Consequently, Roberts continues, "the words for the attitude of the members toward the elders are those of deference and submission to their reasoned leading, and not of obedience (*kupakon*, Cf. Eph. 6:1). Jesus said no one was to exercise authority/rule (*kalepsousiadzo*) in the church (Matt. 25:20)" (p. 56). Their influence is one set by example, in order to motivate others to do the same. See John H. Elliott, "Elders as Leaders in 1 Peter and the Early Church," *Currents in Theology and Mission* 28, no. 6 (2001): 558.

[34] Coulter, "Christ, the Spirit," 336.

though James does not, strictly speaking, belong to the body of apostles appointed by Jesus."[35]

As we zero in on the Council of Jerusalem (Acts 15), we are made aware that along with James, Paul, and Barnabas, the elders were a part of the equation (Acts 15:2, 4, 6). This group of men had to discern once and for all the question, "Do you have to become a Jew before you become a Christian?" In other words, does circumcision assiduously precede faith in Christ to validate one's spiritual journey? This became without question the foremost doctrinal issue of the early church, and they needed to get it right.

Upon significant deliberation, the group, including the elders, recommended that Paul and Barnabas be sent to the Gentile leaders in Antioch, Syria, and Cilicia so that they would be troubled no more with the Law of Moses in having to bear the mark of circumcision as a requirement to faith. The overwhelming catalysis for the decision was the Holy Spirit: "For it seemed good to the Holy Spirit and to us to lay no greater burden on you than these few requirements…" (Acts 15:28).

It remains obvious from the text that the elders were a part of the protocol in arriving at this final decision. And that protocol was the direct leading of the Holy Spirit in making the decision. In addition, the New Testament documents were written well after Pentecost by disciples who couldn't imagine ministry separated from a gift-based platform (1 Cor. 12–14; Eph. 4, Rom. 12; 1 Peter 4:10). They were obviously committed to a church grounded in the same pattern. For the elders and the senior leaders, moving in the Holy Spirit meant moving in the gifts, all with an eye to the upbuilding of the body of Christ. Indeed, their function was for the sake and welfare of the community at large.[36]

---

[35] Coulter, "Christ, the Spirit," 336.
[36] Rob Muthiah, "Charismatic Leadership in the Church: What the Apostle Paul Has to Say to Max Weber," *Journal of Religious Leadership* 9,

The Place of Elders in Earliest Christianity

For the last 120 years, scholarship has been heavily influenced by the work of the German scholar Rudolf Sohm (1841–1917). His understanding of early Christianity with respect to ecclesiology has become a so-called consensus view, largely among Protestant scholars.[37] To give summary to this "consensus view," one has to weed through an enormous amount of material filled with dissenting caveats. However, in broad strokes the "consensus view" goes something like this: the elders in the New Testament were bearers of an office taken from the synagogue matrix. Sohm saw these recipients of Jewish religious culture more prone to operating by law than by grace, and this eventually migrated into the highly rigid Catholic ecclesiology of the third- and fourth-century's church.

In earliest Christianity, people lived in extended families, and in those families the older man (mature male) rose to the position of elder. Furthermore, to understand the early Christian church, one must understand the Jewish world into which it was born. That world was patriarchal, hierarchical, and status driven. However, when the church began to branch out into the unknown regions of the Gentile world, a new understanding began to evolve with the DNA of a charismatic church body, as evidenced in the Pauline churches. Here, the elders were not an "office" among Jewish hierarchy, but more of a rank. They enjoyed a position of honor in the assembled gathering because they were senior members of a primary character. They were distinguished by their service and character.[38]

Now in the charismatic Gentile church, the elders had to function not on a platform of status but on gifting, because the entire church is governed by gifting. The bishops presided over

---

no. 2 (2010): 15.
[37] Alastair Campbell, *The Elders* (Edinburgh: T & T Clark, 1974), 3.
[38] Campbell, *The Elders*, 9.

the Eucharist, and the elders occupied seats of honor with the bishop at the Eucharistic table.[39] Hans von Campenhausen, one of Sohm's protégées, developed this line of thinking concerning the charismatic nature of the church. Von Campenhausen "believed that Paul had an understanding of the church that was at variance with anything that preceded or followed him."[40] "The organizing principle was the "idea of the Spirit who enables different members of the church to function in whatever way was needed";[41] as the body ministry operating in a spiritual gift matrix. In addition, "the moral factors that propel people into positions of power and influence did not operate in the Pauline churches."[42]

Paul's churches were operated on the basis of gospel, not law. For Paul, the church was a body, and each member had an important place to serve. The body functions as the members all contribute, coordinated by the head, which is Christ. So for Paul, the body assembled was a "free fellowship developing through the living interplay of spiritual gifts and ministries without benefit of official authority."[43] In the volatile world of the first century, the Jewish Christian leaders and the Gentile Christian leaders did have points of tension, as we see in Acts 15. It was only through mental submission to the Holy Spirit that they could continue an unfettered gospel in the ancient world. This then became the "consensus view" of Christian scholarship for understanding early-church ecclesiology for Sohm to James Dunn, J. B. Lightfoot, Baur, Ritschl, Hatch, and others well into the twentieth century.

---

[39] Campbell, *The Elders*, 9.
[40] Campbell, *The Elders*, 9.
[41] Campbell, *The Elders*, 11.
[42] Campbell, *The Elders*, 12.
[43] Campbell, *The Elders*, 16.

In the last twenty-five years, an alternative understanding has risen from a group of scholars, which is summarized by John H. Elliott in a review article written in 2003 entitled "Elders as Honored Household Heads and Not Holders of 'Office' in Earliest Christianity." The title becomes the thesis in this instance. After recapping Rudolph Sohm's take on early Christianity, Mr. Elliott clarifies an opposing view examining the New Testament house churches in the society of the Greco-Roman world. His contention is that Sohm and his followers have interpreted their position of New Testament history largely through Protestant Reformation eyes, and to clearly understand it, one needs to step back and view the early church as a society within its own social world very different from our own, a world still fresh with prevailing Jewish cultural assumptions as well as Greco-Roman legal realities.[44]

Dr. Elliott's review of R. Alastair Campbell's *The Elders* has been a kind of "gold standard" for the alternative view of eldership in the New Testament among recent scholars. In their way of thinking, elders were never "holders of office in the church, but like elders everywhere, were always persons of leading households and clans who were honored in their communities as 'senior members of proven Christian character.'"[45] After focusing on elders in Israel, Campbell concludes, "'The elders' is a collective term for the leadership of the tribe or ruling class, but never the title of an office to which an individual might be appointed."[46] They are the "senior men of community, heads of leading families within it, who as such

---

[44] Campbell, *The Elders*, 18.
[45] John H. Elliott, "Elders as Honored Household Heads and Not Holders of 'Office' in Earliest Christianity," *Biblical Theological Bulletin: A Journal of Bible and Theology* 28, no. 6 (2001): 71.
[46] Elliott, "Elders as Honored," 77.

exercise an authority that is informal, representative, and collective."[47] In this understanding, "Eldership connotes not only age, but also wisdom and honor deriving from the prestige of the families whose heads they were."[48] And with this line of thinking, "*presbyteroi* and *episkopoi* should be viewed as virtually synonymous terms for household heads, with the former term indicating status and the latter term, function."[49]

Campbell uses evidence from the book of Acts, which he considers historically reliable, to again refer to "elders" as a collective group who represent individual households. When these men are "appointed (Acts 14:23), they are not ordained to an office, but the appointment is more of a blessing."[50] How he knows that is a puzzlement to this author. This may be true, but they were also at least appointed to a "function," which would be recognized by the church and issue in an ongoing leadership role, hence an elder. When the term *episkopos* was used in the Pastoral letters, it was a somewhat superior designation in terms of function over the elder or deacon, as far as Dr. Campbell is

---

[47] Elliott, "Elders as Honored," 78.
[48] Elliott, "Elders as Honored," 78. Dr. Elliott goes on to say, "This leadership by elders should not be seen as a pattern borrowed from the synagogue as a replacement for charismatic leaders following Paul (contra the consensus view), but as a natural development as their status as respected heads of the households in which the believers assembled for worship from the very outset of the messianic movement."
[49] Elliott, "Elders as Honored," 78. To fill out the picture, Elliott goes on to say, "As the number of individual house churches increased and the individual *episkopos*/overseers gathered for deliberation, they eventually were identified *collectively* as 'the elders', i.e., *episkopoi* considered together and acting corporately. [T]he title 'the elders' was not used in the first generation when churches were small and confined to one household, but appeared in the second generation when 'leaders of house'—churches would need to relate and act together in a *representative* (and collective) capacity."
[50] Elliott, "Elders as Honored," 78.

concerned. However, Gordon Fee takes issue with this line of thinking because he maintains that the Pastorals were not directed to issues of church order in general, but rather to address and correct a single historical situation of elders who were straying from the faith and promulgating false teaching. As he says, "These leaders were persisting in sin and needed to be publicly exposed and rebuked (1 Tim. 5:10) so that others would take warning."[51]

According to Dr. Fee and others, whether the elders to whom Timothy and Titus gave leadership were "heads of households" or not, the pattern seems to be that they were appointed by Paul (Acts 14:23) some years earlier in Ephesus and that the term "elders" is probably a covering term for both overseer and deacons (1 Thess. 3:2, 8; Titus 1:7), and in all cases the leadership was plural.[52] These leaders were plural in nature and were appointed to "rule" (*hoi proistamenoi*) (1 Thess. 5:12; Rom. 12:8) by

---

[51] Gordon D. Fee "Reflections on Church Order as the Pastoral Epistles, with Further Reflections on the Hermeneutics of *ad hoc* Documents," *Journal of the Evangelical Theological Society* 28, no. 2 (1985): 146. Dr. Fee continues to explain: "What we can envision, therefore, on the basis of all the evidence is a scene in which the various house churches each had one or more elders. The issue therefore was not so much that a large gathered assembly was being split down the middle as that various house churches were capitulating almost all together to its leadership that had gone astray (e.g. Gnosticism /Hellenistic Judaism). The letter betrays evidence everywhere that it was intended for the church itself, not just Timothy. Because of defections in the leadership, Paul does not, as before, write directly to the church, but to the church through Timothy. The reason for going this route would have been twofold: 1) to encourage Timothy himself to carry out this most difficult task of stopping the erring elders, who had become thoroughly disputatious, and 2) to authorize Timothy before the church to carry out the task. At the same time, of course, the church will be having the false teachers/teachings exposed before them."
[52] Fee "Reflections," 147.

Apostolic authority in the churches.[53] All the evidence seems to fly in the face of the theory of Campbell and others.

This study takes the position that the early church elders could have been both honored heads of households and designated apostolic appointees to function in an oversight relationship to the early church. Dr. Fee flatly states that at least two aspects of the ministry of elders during this period were for certain: 1) "The elders called overseers were responsible for teaching (1 Tim. 3:3, 5:17; Titus 1: 9), for which they were to receive remuneration (1 Tim. 5:17), and 2) the elders together were responsible for 'managing' or 'caring for' the local church (see 1 Tim. 3:4-5; 5:17), whatever that might have involved at that time in history."[54]

Again, at least in the larger cities, we are looking at a plurality of leadership (multiple elders) among the house churches, who find themselves as key players in the ongoing maintenance of the early church. In this, they are accountable to God (Heb. 13:17), the Apostolic mentors (1 Tim. 1:3-4), and the church fellowship where they serve (1 Tim. 5:19). They are the key cog in the wheel of earliest Christianity as the church progressively crosses many boundaries and geographical areas in its outreach to the ancient world.

Elders in First Peter

In 1 Peter 5:1-5, we find a curious "cluster of vocabulary and

---

[53] Fee "Reflections," 147.
[54] Fee "Reflections," 148. An amazing insight that makes the situation in the Pastorals even more grave is further explained by Dr. Fee: "In contrast to Galatians and 2 Corinthians, there is not a hint in 1 or 2 Timothy, that the False Teachers are outsiders. In fact everything points to their being insiders. They clearly function as teachers (1 Tim. 1:3; 6:7; 6:3); they have themselves wandered away from and made shipwreck of their faith (Tim. 1:6, 19); and two of them are named and have been excommunicated (1 Tim. 1:20). Since teaching is the one clearly expressed duty of the elders (1 Tim. 3:3; 5:17), it follows naturally that the false teachers were already teachers—thus elders—who have gone astray."

images (elders, overseers/exercise oversight, shepherds, flock) representing a growing coalescence of terms for leaders and their functions in the early Jesus movement."[55]

Dr. Elliott begins by acknowledging that 1 Peter 4:7-11 is a significant mention of *charismata,* "however it has no relevance to the issue of leadership or to charismatic forms of authority, however much this has been assumed in earlier scholarship."[56] His reasoning is because this pericope is addressed to the entire community, encouraging a corporate action through *charismata* to struggle against a hostile society. I would challenge such reasoning precisely because the leaders mentioned in 1 Peter 5:1-5 are a part of the entire community, and if they are called upon to be an example to the larger flock (1 Peter 5:3), then they too would yield themselves to the leading of the Holy Spirit and His gifts. After all it was Peter who was an original disciple, and who then became an original apostle and was present at Pentecost when the power of the Holy Spirit was conferred on all assembled (Acts 2:1-4). Furthermore, it was there at Pentecost that Peter alluded to Isaiah 59:20-21, where the promise of the Spirit would "not depart out of your mouth or out of the mouth of your children, or out of your children's children from this time forth and for evermore." [57] And Peter confirmed this word in Acts 2:39. Given the history, one would think it unthinkable for Peter to deny such Spirit (*charismata*) activity when instructing the churches in his purview, just a decade or two after Pentecost.

Dr. Elliott then acknowledges that the dissemination of Elders Ministry is all over the board, noted in the earliest Jerusalem

---

[55] Elliott, "Elders as Leaders," 549. Dr. Elliott goes on to say that the text of 1 Peter remains "one of the earliest witnesses to this constellation and its symbolization of community leaders as elders-pastors-overseers."
[56] Elliott, "Elders as Leaders," 550.
[57] Isaiah 59: 21.

church (Acts 11:30; 15:4, 6, 22, 23; 16:4; 21:18), as well as the appointment by Paul and Barnabas on their first missionary journey (Acts 14:23); and now Peter's own letter directed to the saints in Asia Minor and attested by several others (Acts 20:17; 1 Tim. 5:17-22; 2 Jn. 1:3; 3 Jn: 1), as well as letters by Ignatius, Polycarp, and 1 Clement.[58]

Two issues among many that Dr. Elliott lifts out for our study in 1 Peter and that are significant for the conclusion of this study are the role of elders in exercising oversight as in (*poimen*) "shepherd," which involves a responsibility of safeguarding the flock, and the very important emphasis on humility (1 Peter 5:5), which is crucial for any argument for modern-day elders in the twenty-first century.[59]

First let us look at the role of the shepherd. "The depiction of God's people as a 'flock' or as 'sheep' under the guidance and care of God or human leaders as 'shepherds' *poimenes* (*poimainein*) has familiar Old Testament roots."[60] In addition, Jesus referred to the pastoral metaphor both with respect to Himself and His disciples (Mk. 6:34; Mt. 9:36; Jn. 10:1-18). Jesus actually commissioned Peter personally to step into this role in an ongoing manner following His exit (Jn. 21:15-17). We also see allusions to this metaphor throughout the New Testament in Acts 20:28 and Ephesians 4:11, as well as the Apostle Paul's farewell address at Miletus to the elders of Ephesus (Acts 20:17-35).[61] When this function of shepherd is mandated for effective eldership and used interchangeably with *episkopos*, it simply yields strength to the argument that elders are an extension of the pastor or appointed senior leader in any church fellowship. Dr. Elliott's summary statement is perspicuous:

---

[58] Elliott, "Elders as Leaders," 554.
[59] Elliott, "Elders as Leaders," 554 and 559, respectively.
[60] Elliott, "Elders as Leaders," 554.
[61] Elliott, "Elders as Leaders," 555.

56 Biblical Eldership

> 1 Peter and Acts, both composed in the final third of the first century, provide the earliest evidence of a developing trend to attribute to elders the function of oversight and to portray elders and overseers as shepherds of the flock. Three terms are brought together here—elders (*presbyteroi*), overseers (*episkopoi*), and shepherds (*poimenes, poimainein*)—in a manner that indicates their initial synonymous use as designations for Christian leaders.[62]

The second characteristic attached to this level of leadership in the early church, which will bring us to our conclusion, is that of humility. Peter says in 1 Peter 5:5b, "Clothe yourselves, all of you, with humility toward one another, for God opposes the proud, but gives the grace to the humble." This is amazing instruction coming from a man who healed a man lame from birth at the gate of the Temple in Acts 3:1; and who opposed the threats and intimidations in Jerusalem of Annas, the High Priest, and Caiaphas, along with other high-ranking Jewish and secular officials in Acts 4:19-20; and who on another occasion in Solomon's Portico allowed the sick and infirm even to glance at his shadow and be healed (Acts 5:15-16). One would think that a man of this caliber would walk with a bit of a swagger; but apparently not Peter. There are only two gravitational pulls on a person of this status: inflated ego or extreme humility. Peter chooses the latter and taught his fellow elders the same. As Dr. Elliott has said, "Elders, like slaves (2:18-25), wives (3:4), and all the believers (3:8; 5:5b-7), are to exemplify in their lives and conduct the humility manifested by the Christ (2:21-23), for humility is a fundamental characteristic of those favored by God."[63]

---

[62] Elliott, "Elders as Leaders," 555.
[63] Elliott, "Elders as Leaders," 559.

Conclusion

In the beginning of this literature review, it was stated that most churches and denominations employ some form of elder ministry in the administration of their ecclesiastical protocol. Nearly every denominational structure is linked into a particular ecclesiology by virtue of its progressive history. Most all import elements of the original New Testament model, but few if any seem to have a "pure" New Testament model. All claim to be biblical, yet in many cases, significant differences remain.

For our purpose, a simple New Testament model may give expression to a renewed pattern of leadership, at least in my denomination, the UMC, especially when said pattern is wed to a charismatic gift-based milieu. Locked up in the scripture and the Spirit of God are all the tools we need for effective ministry. In the author's experience at the parish level, frustrations and challenges grew not because of internal power struggles with the congregation or ineptness of the pastor, or a hundred other reasons why pressure invades the ministry context. No, it was because I was actually doing something right and congregational growth was exceeding all of our expectations. The church was responding to my leadership, and I was being led to develop a whole different kind of UMC.

Apparently I was ahead of my time, because years ago I received some persecution (using the word lightly) over things that have become standard fare in the UMC today, such as contemporary worship, creative evangelism, satellite locations, and more. I cried out to the Lord, and God answered the prayer of desperation. This project asserts what God did for me, He will do for others. If only through introspection and self-evaluation initiated by the Holy Spirit, a renewed leadership protocol stands on the horizon for all who would embrace it.

3

Theoretical Foundation

WHEN WE BEGIN WITH THE BIBLE, we must begin with the Old Testament. It is there that the locus of God's original interaction with man is revealed. In this chapter we will look at the biblical writers' understanding of eldership portrayed in both testaments. In addition, we will also survey the historical evidence for Biblical Eldership primarily within the first 300 years of the church and explain how the New Testament concept migrated into something unrecognizable to the first witnesses. Finally, we will surmise the theological implications of the former two for the church in the twenty-first century.

Biblical Foundation

From the biblical record there seems to be sufficient evidence that the concept of elder ministry found its basis and use in the Old Testament Jewish synagogue matrix.[64] Furthermore, the biblical

---

[64] "The thought of eldership is very prominent in the Old Testament. A consideration of these following references reveals a progressive

evidence suggests a measure of the Spirit of God that was enhanced for leadership relative to eldership both in Israel and in the Church.

We begin with the picture of Moses in the wilderness with the newly released people of Israel. They face a very critical juncture in their journey from the wilderness of Sinai (Exod. 10:12) to the wilderness of Paran (Exod. 12:16) and points west into the Promised Land. When one takes the wide-angle lens on the larger narrative of Israel's wanderings in the wilderness, one would see that it actually begins at Exodus 13:17 and continues through the end of Deuteronomy, while encompassing the literary context for our text.[65]

In the Numbers 11:16-30 pericope, Moses is given instruction by God to appoint seventy elders of the people to help him govern an increasingly disgruntled people. Most anyone familiar with church leadership will recognize this as a perennial problem. The issue on this occasion was one of food, particularly meat, which had been absent from their diet since leaving Egypt. The people question Moses's leadership, and he goes to God uttering a plaint while the people utter their complaint.[66] Moses

---

development of the concept of eldership from Patriarchal Eldership to Political and Ecclesiastical Eldership. These elders were men of age, of experience and of authority. Sometimes great men are not always wise and younger sometimes are (Eccles. 4:13; Psalms 119:99)," Kevin J. Conner, *The Church in the New Testament* (Portland, OR: City Bible Publishing, 1982), 87. See also: Gen. 50:7; Prov. 31:23; Exod. 3:16, 18, 4:29; 12:21, 17:5, 7, 18:12; 19:7, 24:1, 9, 14; Lev. 4:15; Num. 22:7, 11:16-30; Deut. 5:23, 19:12, 21:1-20, 22:15-18, 25:7-9; Judges 8:16; 2 Sam. 19:11; 2 Kings 19:2; 1 Chron. 11:3, 15:25; 2 Chron. 19:8-11; Ruth 4:2; Ezra 10:14; Isa. 37:2; Psalms 107:32.

[65] Frederick C. Tiffany and Sharon H. Ringe, *Biblical Interpretation: A Roadmap* (Nashville, TN: Abingdon Press, 1996), 131.

[66] James Philip, *The Communicator's Commentary: Numbers*, ed. Lloyd J. Ogilvie (Waco, TX: Word Books, Publisher, 1987), 139.

is actually experiencing "sheep bite," a common problem experienced among God's pastoral leaders. With so many people to lead and care for, Moses is not sure he is up to the task. However, God must know better because Moses is given the instruction to appoint elders.

Here we are witnessing "the beginning of an administrative structure to address the social needs of this people with its own emerging identity and common life."[67] What so fascinates me here is that God's remedy for Moses's predicament comes in the form of a spiritual anointing rather than an analytical/functional design. Instead, an anointing or a divine enablement (*ruach*[68]) was present. And as one scholar has said, "We are not to understand this as implying, that the fullness of the Spirit possessed by Moses was diminished in consequence."[69] (As did John Calvin.[70]) "For the Spirit of God is not something material, which is diminished by being divided, but resembles a flame of fire, which does not decrease in intensity, but increases rather by extension."[71] So Moses assembled the elders at the Tabernacle to receive God's promised Spirit.[72]

In addition, an interesting caveat in this sequence of scripture is that two of these elders did not go to the Tabernacle with the others for the "impartation." And yet these two were anointed

---

[67] Tiffany and Ringe, *Biblical Interpretation*, 135.
[68] Gregory A. Lent, ed., *Leviticus–Numbers*, vol. 3, *The Complete Biblical Library: The Old Testament* (Springfield, MO; World Library Press, 1995), 436.
[69] C. F. Keil and Franz Delitzsch, eds., *Old Testament Commentaries* (Grand Rapids, Associated Publishers and Authors, 1971), 1:805.
[70] John Calvin, *Commentary on the Harmony of the Pentateuch* (London: Calvin Translation Society, 1845), 4:25.
[71] Keil and Delitzsch, *Old Testament Commentaries*, 1:805.
[72] Notice the parallels with the New Testament outpouring of the Holy Spirit, only to be received after the 120 gathered at a pre-appointed location to wait on the gracious empowerment from God (Acts 2:1–4).

with the Spirit of God and prophesied just as the others. We are not told the reason for their absence. However, when a protest was voiced in lieu of this, Moses's response is very key: "Would that all the Lord's people were prophets, that the Lord would put his spirit on them" (Num. 11:29). Perhaps Moses was able to foresee a day when a universal prophethood would be evidenced among God's people.[73] Other Old Testament prophets foresaw such a day.[74]

So being anointed and led by the Holy Spirit would become the pattern for this new nation, and that would carry the day. They simply were a led people. This is further confirmed by the image of the ark of the covenant (Num. 35-36) and the language of the cloud (which led Israel during the daylight hours) (Num. 10; 11-12, 34), conveying the notion of divine guidance and leadership as well as offering assurance that the promise will be fulfilled, that the journey will lead to the Promised Land.[75]

"Moses' wish for a universal outpouring of the Spirit of prophecy denied the elitist tendency to develop religious hierarchies and to restrict special divine graces to leaders; it seems to anticipate the ideal of the Messianic bestowal of the Spirit as portrayed by the New Testament" (Mk. 1:8; Matt. 3:11; Lk. 3:16; Jn. 7:37; Acts 1:5).[76] One can surmise that at least some of the intimacy that Moses had developed with *YHWH* was exemplified in the lives of the seventy elders. This is precisely what I have experienced in my ministry in the local church,

---

[73] Dale Moody, *The Spirit of the Living God* (Philadelphia, PA: Westminster Press, 1968), 32.
[74] See: Joel 2:28; Isa. 59:21; Ezek. 36:26, 37:14; Zech. 12:10; Jer. 31:31-34; Lk. 24:49.
[75] Tiffany and Ringe, *Biblical Interpretation*, 141.
[76] Mark Virkler, Gary S. Greig, Mike Rogers, and Maurice Fuller, *Heavenly Encounters: As We Pray and Worship Before the Throne*, An Abstract (2012, A Thesis on Prophetic Gesture), 57.

which I believe is conducive to our present spiritual environment in the twenty-first century. Let us explore this further in the New Testament.

New Testament Understandings

We now turn our attention to the church in the New Testament with an emphasis on church order (ecclesiology) through the local church expression.[77] Particular reference will be given to the example of elders and bishops during the period A.D. 50 to 100.[78] The following inquiry will also take us to such considerations as the role of the prophetic in eldership, the laying on of hands through commissioning, and the necessary qualifications as well as the duties of the New Testament elder in order to arrive at a general "all purpose" pattern of New Testament church order as well as division of responsibilities.

We begin by saying that "leadership by a council of elders is a form of government found in nearly every society of the ancient Near East. It was the foundational governmental structure of the nation of Israel throughout its Old Testament history (Exod. 3:16; Ezra 10:8). For Israel, a tribal, patriarchal society, the eldership structure was as basic as the family. So when the New Testament records that Paul, a Jew who was thoroughly immersed in the Old Testament and Jewish culture, appointed elders for his newly founded churches (Acts 14:23), it means that he

---

[77] Eduard Schweizer reminds us that the structure that eventually became the order of leadership in the New Testament was a "witness" unto itself. He says, "The New Testament's pronouncements on Church order are to be read as a *gospel*—that is, Church order is to be regarded as a part of the proclamation in which the church's witness is expressed, as it is in its preaching." Eduard Schweizer, *Church Order in the New Testament* (Eugene, OR; Wipf & Stock Publishers, 1961), 14.
[78] Alan Richardson, *A Theological Wordbook of the Bible* (New York: The MacMillan Company, 1950), 150.

established a council of elders in each local church."[79] As a result, we recognize from the outset the Jewish roots to the pattern of eldership in the New Testament churches.[80]

However, the New Testament pattern for eldership did not purely come from an Old Testament template superimposed by Jesus. There were similarities but also many differences, some of which we will cover. As we consider the nuances of the leadership designation "elders" in the New Testament church, we must remember that the leadership constructs came directly from Jesus Christ and not tradition (Matt. 28:16-20). Paul in Ephesus speaks of our common access to the Father through the Holy Spirit, with being a household built on the foundation of the Apostles and prophets, Christ Jesus Himself being the cornerstone (Eph. 2:18-22). In other words the twelve apostles were the governmental and foundational supervisors of the early church. In a natural progression through time, their leadership was turned over to local church leaders who became the local ruling authorities (servants/elders) in the church at large.[81] It is, however, important to realize that the designation "elder" is always in the plural form when tied to church leadership, even

---

[79] Alexander Strauch, *Biblical Eldership: An Urgent Call to Restore Biblical Church Leadership* (Littleton, CO: Lewis & Roth Publishers, 1995), 39.

[80] "In establishing elders, the Christian church was following the organization of the Jewish church all over the Roman Empire. The affairs of the local Jewish synagogue were in the hands of a body of elders who conducted its business and exercised discipline in accordance with Mosaic Law. There is evidence that these Jewish elders were appointed to their office by the laying on of hands." Richardson, *A Theological Wordbook*, 149.

[81] "Although the apostles outranked the elders in authority, the elders were destined to become the highest permanent officers in the church." E. J. Carnell, *The Case for Biblical Christianity: Essays on Theology, Philosophy, Ethics, Ecumenism, Fundamentalism, Separatism* (Grand Rapids: William B. Eerdmans Publishing Co., 1969), 164.

though no set number of elders is mentioned and the designation "church" is always in the singular form when tied to the ministry of elders in a particular city.[82]

The Apostle Paul's appointment of elders (Acts 14:23) encompassed a group of individuals who equally shared authority, responsibility, and leadership in a local church assembly. We are definitely speaking of a plurality of leadership who met specific moral and spiritual qualifications before they served (1 Tim. 3:1-7; Titus 1:5-9); who were publically examined by the church as to these qualifications (1 Tim. 3:10); who were publicly installed in office (1 Tim. 5:22; Acts 14:23); and who were empowered by the Holy Spirit to do their work.[83] This pattern of shared leadership is consistent throughout the New Testament.[84] Furthermore, the team effort of leadership includes but is not limited to: oversight/ management[85], preaching and teaching[86], protecting the church from false teachers[87], exhorting and admonishing the church as to sound doctrine[88], visiting the sick and praying for healing[89], judging doctrinal issues[90], and dealing with church discipline and apostasy.[91] The motivation for this

---

[82] See Kevin Connor, *The Church in the New Testament,* 96. The reason for the singular form for church is because Paul's letters were addressed to cities, not individual congregations in a city. However, the leadership of the church in a particular city was a plurality of leadership, hence the word "elders."
[83] Strauch, *Biblical Eldership,* 39.
[84] See: Acts 13:1, 15:35; 1 Cor. 16:15-16; 1 Thess. 5:12-13; Heb. 13:7, 17, 24.
[85] Acts 20:28; Titus 1:7; 1 Peter 5:2-3.
[86] Heb. 13:7; Tim. 5:17; Titus 1:9; 1 Tim. 3:2; 2 Tim. 2:2.
[87] Acts 15, 20:7, 28:31; Acts 2:42, 16:4-5; 1 Tim. 4:1.
[88] Acts 20:17, 28; 1 Peter 5:2; John 21:15-17.
[89] James 5:14-15; Eph. 3:4; Jer. 23:1-5.
[90] Acts 15:22-31; Rom. 16:17-18; Col. 2:8, 18; 1 Cor. 1:10-16.
[91] 1 Tim. 3:14-15.

entire ministry is love and concern for God's flock.[92] Proverbs 27:23 says, "Know well the condition of your flock, and give attention to your herds."

Defining Terms in the New Testament Church

The terms "bishop" and "elder" for the most part seem to be interchangeable terms in the New Testament. The term bishop is *episkopos* in Greek, which means "overseer, a superintendent, a guardian."[93] The term carries with it the connotation of shepherding; as Paul says in Acts 20:28, "Take heed to yourselves and to all the flock, in which the Holy Spirit has made you overseers, to care for the church of God, which he obtained with the blood of his own Son." The term is also used of Jesus in 1 Peter 2:25, so it carries significant weight. [94] What is interesting is that even though the shepherding aspect is addressed to bishops in general, the section within which it occurs (Acts 20:17) is addressed to elders.

The term *elder* (Gk. *presbyteros*) means "elder," "older person," or "a senior."[95] The term *elder* was probably the most common

---

[92] Strauch, *Biblical Eldership*, 16.
[93] Connor, *The Church in the New Testament*, 105.
[94] "In the course of the 2nd century there came to be a single bishop in each city or district, who was recognized as a 'successor' of the apostles and as alone possessing, like the apostles, all the powers of the Christian ministry. Each bishop was himself consecrated to his office by other bishops, and he alone ordained others to the lesser ministries or 'orders' of presbyters and deacons." Richardson, *A Theological Wordbook*, 152.
[95] "The term *presbyteros* carries a twofold sense as a designation for age and a title for office. In a few contexts it is hard to know which of these designations is intended, but in most cases the intended meaning is clear. Depending on the context, then, *presbyteros* can mean: (1) 'older man' or 'old man', as in 1 Tim: 1:5: 'Do not sharply rebuke an older man (*presbyteroi*)' or (2) a title for a community official, an 'elder,' as in 1 Tim.

term in the New Testament when speaking of local church leadership. These were the leaders where the "rubber meets the road," so to speak. They were generally all-purpose "rulers" who gave guidance, direction, and stability to the assembled saints. The following passage from 1 Peter 5:1-5 gives the reader a good introduction to the care and leadership displayed in the elder:

> So exhort the elders among you, as a fellow elder and a witness of the sufferings of Christ as well as a partaker in the glory that is to be revealed. Tend the flock of God that is your charge, not by constraint but willingly, not for shameful gain but eagerly, not as domineering over those in your charge but being examples to the flock. And when the chief shepherd is manifested you will obtain the unfading crown of glory. Likewise you that are younger be subject to the elders. Clothe yourselves, all of you, with humility toward one another, for God opposes the proud, but gives grace to the humble.[96]

Having said this, let us not forget "all the various ministerial

---

5:17: 'Let the elders (*presbyteroi*) who rule well be considered worthy of double honor. Although the strict sense of advanced age is eliminated from the meaning of elder when referring to a community leader, certain connotations such as maturity, experience, dignity, authority, and honor are retained. Thus the term *elder* conveys positive concepts of maturity, respect, and wisdom. When *presbyteros* is used of a community leader, it is most commonly used in the plural form, *presbyteroi*. This is because the elder structure of leadership is leadership by a council of elders." Strauch, *Biblical Eldership,* 125.

[96] "Each metaphor emphasizes a particular aspect of God's Church and, of course, is limited in its ability to portray all dimensions of the Church. So the image of the church as a flock must not be isolated from other biblical images such as pillar and support of the truth, holy priesthood, the temple of God, household of God, body of Christ, an holy nation. When these diverse images are placed together, however, they set forth a balanced and glorious picture of the Church's multidimensional nature." Strauch, *Biblical Eldership,* 243.

functions by which the life of the church is maintained and extended, are 'gifts' (Gk. *charismata*, gift of Holy grace), of Christ to the church through the presence and operation of the Holy Spirit within it."[97] These gifts are delineated in four principal sections of the New Testament (1 Cor. 12-14; Eph. 4:1-11; Rom. 12:6-9, and 1 Peter 4:10[98]).

First Among Equals

Since this project establishes a need for Biblical Eldership to come alongside the pastor, where does the pastor fit into this matrix? 1 Timothy 5:17 sets the pace for an elder gifted with pastoral graces. It states, "Let the elders who rule well be considered of double honor, especially those who labor in preaching and teaching." As Alexander Strauch so aptly says:

> Although elders act jointly as a council and share equal authority and responsibility for the leadership of the church, all are not equal in their giftedness, biblical knowledge, leadership ability, experience, or dedication. Therefore, those among the elders who are particularly gifted leaders and/or teachers will naturally stand out among the other elders and leaders within the leadership body. This is what the Romans called *primus inter paces*, meaning "first among equals."[99]

I believe Kevin Connor makes an excellent point in this regard when he says, "God's form of government is *theocratic in character*. This is to say God *chooses, calls,* and *equips* certain persons to be rulers and leaders over his people, investing and

---

[97] Richardson, *A Theological Wordbook,* 147.
[98] "The one thing that does not change every time the word *charisma* is used in the New Testament is that these gifts are given for the building up of the body. Either it is an escape of Paul from a shipwreck or the gifts he writes about in 1 Corinthians 14, they are all *charismata* and they are always for building up the church in some way." Mark Dever, *Nine Marks of a Healthy Church* (Wheaton, IL: Crossway Books, 2000), 220.
[99] Strauch, *Biblical Eldership,* 45.

delegating them with *degrees of authority* according to his will. These persons are most commonly called elders. This does not exalt this elder above the others, but sets him in responsibility as 'First among equals.'"[100] As a result, their particular "gift package" made them eligible for a strategic function in the Body of Christ.

There remains ample precedent in the New Testament for "first among equals" within the ranks of the apostles and disciples. The concept is demonstrated among Jesus's disciples in Luke 8:51, 9:28 and Mark 14:33 with respect to Peter, James, and John. Among these three, Peter is the "first among equals." In four separate lists of disciples, Peter's name is first: Matthew 10:2-4, Mark 3:16-19, Luke 6:4-16, and Acts 1:13. In addition, in all four Gospels, Peter is the prominent figure among the twelve. Jesus charged Peter at one point to "strengthen your brothers" (Lk. 22:32). Paul also acknowledges Peter, James, and John as "pillars" of the church in Jerusalem (Gal. 2:7-9).[101]

---

[100] Connor, *The Church*, 92. In addition, the precedent was set for this particular concept prior to the New Testament elder. For example there were: (a) "chief priests" among the priesthood (Lk. 9:22, 20:1); (b) "chief Pharisees among the Pharisees (Lk. 14:1); (c) "chief rulers of the Synagogue" (Acts 18:8, 17); (d) "chief apostles among the apostles" (2 Cor. 11:5, 12:11); (e) "chief musicians" in the Tabernacle of David, who were also chief of the Levites (1 Chron. 15:22; Psalms 4, 5, 6 Titles); (f) Michael is called "chief archangel" amongst the angelic orders (Daniel 10:13), Connor, 92. In addition we are reminded that "the thing the 'chief elder' has to be aware of is that Diotrephes spirit and attitude, the desire to have the pre-eminence. He has to truly recognize that he himself is an elder among elders, and NOT an elder ABOVE other elders." Connor, *The Church*, 94. As was quoted above, Peter keys us in on this most important emphasis within this entire process of leadership, and that is "humility." The thought is even carried over into a "cosmic level" with the structure of the Godhead. God is the FIRST person, Jesus is the SECOND person, and the Holy Spirit is the THIRD person of the Godhead and yet there is no competition with one another, only perfect unity of purpose and will.
[101] Strauch, *Biblical Eldership*, 45-46.

Furthermore, the pattern of "first among equals" continues to hold true with the appointment of the deacons (Gk. *diakonia*), which means service or attendance as a servant.[102] In Acts 6, even though there were seven appointed to serve tables, the two who seem to be prominent are Philip and Stephen (Acts 6:8-7:60; 8:4-40; 21:8). And as we continue we see the concept evidenced with the Apostle Paul and Barnabas, who were commissioned together for the first missionary journey from the church in Antioch (Acts 13:1ff). The sequence begins by recording Barnabas's name first, but as time goes on, Paul rises to the top in prominence with his name being first.[103] If this isn't enough, after Peter leaves Jerusalem, James becomes the senior elder/shepherd in Jerusalem. He presides over and closes the council of Jerusalem in Acts 15.

Alexander Strauch's closing statement concerning "first among equals" seems appropriate at this juncture. "The advantage of the principle 'first among equals' is that it allows for functional, gift based diversity with the eldership team without creating an official superior office over fellow elders."[104]

---

[102] "Jesus Christ, as the Head of the church, gave us the supreme example of Deaconship. This was because he had the spirit and attitude of a Servant. Christ is THE DEACON, THE SERVANT, one among us. He came not be ministered unto but to minister and give His life a ransom for man. He came to serve and act as a Deacon (Mark 10:42-45; Rom. 15:8). He said to the 12 apostles that they would be great if they served one another: 'Whoever would be great among you must be your servant' (Matt. 20:26)." (Conner, *The Church*, 125). A servant heart is the preeminent characteristic as "boots hit the ground" in the service of the Gospel of Jesus Christ. See: Lk. 10:40; Acts 1:17, 25; 6:1, 4; 11:29; 12:25; 20:24; 21:19; Rom. 11:13; 12:7; 15:31; 1 Cor. 12:5; 16:15; 2 Cor. 3:7-9; 4:1; 5:18; 6:3; 8:4; 9:1, 12, 13; 11:8; Eph. 4:12; Col. 4:17; 1 Tim. 1:12; 2 Tim. 4:5, 11; Heb. 1:14; Rev. 2:19.

[103] See: Barnabas and Paul: Acts 11:30, 12:25, 13:2, 13:7, 14:14, 15:2; and then the order switches to Paul and Barnabas: Acts 13:13, 13:43; 13:46, 13:50, 15:2, 15:22, 15:35.

[104] Strauch, *Biblical Eldership*, 48.

Beginning in the second century, the church began to drift into a hierarchical division and really deteriorated after Constantine officially made the entire Roman Empire Christian in A.D. 313. Christianity turned inward rather than outward and became fixated on structure, ceremony, ecclesiology, and basically the subjugation of the layman. The following 1,100 years becomes a distortion of the New Testament concept.

Excursus: Female Leadership in the Church

No one can dispute the strides women have made in the workplace and in the culture over the last fifty years. There have been "strenuous efforts to end discrimination against women, in the workplace, in the home within marriage in respect to property and in their treatment of significant institutions such as banks, building societies, and insurance companies."[105] The need for such reform has come at a high price because of centuries of patriarchal attitudes and actions where men have dominated the female sex and ever exploited her for purposes of power. For the vast history of the race, women have been mere chattel as they negotiated a patriarchal-tribal driven world dominated by men in most every sector of life.

Today we find ourselves in the twenty-first century, and yet, in many parts of the world, women are still oppressed and denied basic human rights. Women are seen and appreciated for their functional characteristics alone, as they are viewed as a kind of property of man. Just in the last few years, the world has witnessed an Afghani woman sent to prison because she was convicted of wearing pants in public. To be sure, women throughout the Middle East live as second-class citizens in a

---

[105] Neil Summerton, *A Noble Task: Eldership & Ministry in the Local Church* (Carlisle, UK: The Paternoster Press, 1994), 133.

continual state of subjugation. When you break it down, it really is about power and control. Many who rule with iron-clad power are never satisfied. The result is exploitation at the expense of others. Imperialism and territorial reach are the malevolent results of endless power quests. One wonders if mankind will ever be free of this kind of havoc and misery. History is replete with examples, and volumes have been written on the subject.

As we study church ecclesiology and the role of eldership in church history, this treatise would be negligent if it failed to address the issue of women and leadership in the church as we move into the twenty-first century. I have included this section to clear the air on the subject, realizing that the question of women in ministry would eventually come up. My position is not necessarily to advocate for women, but to fill in the biblical picture as I see it.

To begin, one must be sufficiently informed as to the religious and cultural attitude preceding and up to the time of Jesus. Neil Summerton in his book, *A Noble Task,* does a fine job summarizing the Jewish milieu. Mr. Summerton says:

> The key question is, are women in creation human beings on a par with men; and in both creation and redemption does God envisage that they may have the same kind of relationship with him as can be enjoyed by men? It is worth noticing that the answer given by the Jewish theologians and religious institutions whom Jesus and the early church addressed was both implicitly and explicitly in the negative. It is a commonplace that women could only advance in the Temple to the court of women, and could not proceed that far while menstruating. In the synagogue women were frequently, if not generally relegated to a separate part of the building and not allowed to take any part in the proceedings. However, many women (slaves and children) were present; there could be no synagogue unless ten free adult men were available. Women

could hear the service, but were not normally allowed to participate. While the men came to learn, women came only to hear. At least one rabbi declined to answer a public question from a woman on the grounds that "there is no wisdom in a woman, except with the distaff": and the Jerusalem commentary on the incident represents the rabbi as explaining, "It is better that the words of the Law should be burned than that they should be given to a woman."

As teachers, women were confined to the teaching of their own children and were not even to be entrusted with the task of teaching others' children. The position was understandable, given that Philo taught "man is informed by reason, woman by feelings." Josephus summed the matter up: "woman is inferior to the man in every way." And in about A.D. 150, Rabbi Judah ben Elai taught that a man was bound to pray daily, "Blessed art thou…who has not made me a heathen,… who hast not made me a woman,…who hast not made me a brutish (illiterate) man."[106]

As we move into the New Testament, we are introduced to specific examples in the Gospels of the view of the rabbis toward women. Three examples should suffice. In John 8:2–10, the scribes and Pharisees bring to Jesus a woman who had been caught in the act of adultery. This must have been a very dramatic moment. The Jewish authorities stipulated that the Law (Lev. 20:10), given to Moses, required her to be stoned to death. The problem here is that the Law actually required both guilty parties to be stoned to death; however, there was no mention of the guilty man. One usually commits adultery in private, hence an absence of accusers. Jesus becomes the woman's trial lawyer. He contradicted what culture said and took up her defense. He did not pander to the injustice of his day as it related to women.

---

[106] Summerton, *A Noble Task,* 135.

With a very creative response (Spirit-led[107]), Jesus disarmed her accusers, and the rabbis were speechless, leaving one by one. When Jesus looked up and said, "Woman, where are they? Has no one condemned you?" She said, "No one, Lord." And Jesus said, "Neither do I condemn you; go, and do not sin again" (Jn. 8:10).

Another example from the religious community in the first century is that women could not be witnesses in a courtroom (Lk. 18:1-3). They were considered fickle, liars, and uneducated.[108] However, the woman in Luke 18 prevailed on the "unjust judge" and was awarded her plea because she simply wore him down. However, I think it insightful that Jesus picked a woman to be His first witness at His resurrection! They were there with their spices and became witnesses to the greatest event in the history of mankind. If you were following tradition, you would not have picked a woman to do this task, especially this task. What a great cultural reversal, directed by Jesus. In the first Garden back in Genesis, there was pain, restriction, and domination from the curse—"your husband shall rule over you" (Gen. 3:16). This curse is apparently reversed with Mary Magdalene. God is serious about putting the Gospel message in the mouths of women.

One more example should suffice. In John 4, Jesus has an extended theological conversation with a strange woman at the well of Samaria. Rabbis did not go to Samaria and have "theological discourse with women in public." To make things

---

[107] Jesus performs exactly as the Prophets said he would. See Isaiah 9:1-3, especially v. 3-4: "He shall not judge by what his eyes see, or decide by what his ears hear; but with righteousness he shall judge the poor, and decide with equity for the meek of the earth...."

[108] William Barclay, *The Letter to the Ephesians: The Daily Study Bible Series* (Philadelphia, PA: The Westminster Press, 1975), 168.

worse, this particular woman had lived with five different men and had been thrown out of five different houses. She had no self-image left. She was now living with some loser headed to repeat her downward cycle.

Jesus is the seventh man to walk into her life. Following an extended conversation, her eyes were opened to the truth and she was transformed on the spot. Jesus upholds her dignity, and she returns to her home village and coaxes everyone to "come, see a man who told me all that I ever did. Can this be the Christ? They went out of the city and were coming to him" (Jn. 4: 29-30). She becomes an effective evangelist (witness) to the power of God's love.[109] In the end, Jesus offered her love and forgiveness.

The idea that women have been prescriptively relegated to a second-class status is not upheld in the biblical narrative at large. J. Lee Grady reminds us:

> [T]he essence [of] this low view of woman is rooted in the misconception that the first female, Eve, was created by God as an inferior creature with deficient physical strength, less astute mental capacities and limited spiritual giftedness and that because of her weakness she was meant to live in a state of subordination to Adam. It is the idea that because Eve was

---

[109] To miss this pattern in scripture is to miss the forest for the trees. Time after time, God empowers women in the Bible. We find Deborah, a prophetess (Judges 4:4); Miriam, a prophetess (Exodus 15:20; Micah 6:4); Huldah, a prophetess (2 Kings 22:14); Esther, an intercessor and deliverer (Esther 4:14); and in the NT, Phoebe, a deacon in Rome (Romans: 16:1-2); Pricilla, who helped to launch the apostolic ministry of Apollos (Acts 18:24-26; Romans 6:3-5); Phillip's daughters, prophetesses (Acts 21:9); Lois and Eunice, teaching Timothy the faith (2 Timothy: 1:5); Chloe, who led a church (1 Corinthians 1:11); Nympha, who hosted a church in her house (Colossians: 4:15); Euodia and Syntyche, female disciples of Paul (Philippians 4:3); and Priscilla and Aquila, who hosted a church in their house and risked their lives with Paul on the apostolic trail (Romans 16:3-4).

deceived by the serpent, she must forever be punished for her disobedience by living in the shadow of her superior male counterpart.[110]

When Jesus enters the picture, the ancient world is thrown into a real quagmire because He consistently upheld the dignity of women. The contrasts between the true biblical narrative and the Jewish religious/cultural picture could not be farther apart. Again Mr. Summerton weighs in with a succinct summary of this dichotomy:

> All this contrasts sharply with the creation account in which man (male and female) was created in the divine image, and to whom (male and female) the stewardship of creation was committed (Gen. 1:26-30). It contrasts with the role given to woman in sharing in the task of creation husbandry (Gen. 2:18-25), and her joint accountability for it—an accountability which itself has implications for woman's status and responsibility in creation (Gen. 3:8, 9, 13). It contrasts with the proverbial ideal of the business-provider (Prov. 31:10-31). It contrasts with Jesus's practice in admitting women to the discipleship band (Lk. 8:1-3); in allowing them to be rabbinical students (Lk. 10:38-42: "One thing is needful. Mary has chosen the good portion which shall not be taken from her, when Martha was concerned to occupy the role traditionally assigned to women); in allowing them to touch him while ritually unclean (Lk. 7:39 and 8:43-48) and in allowing them the most intimate relationship of worship

---

[110] J. Lee Grady, *10 Lies the Church Tells Women* (Lake Mary, FL: Creation House Publishers, 2000), 24. Furthermore, "the fact that Eve was presented to Adam to 'help' him does not make her inferior. On the contrary, God had already said, 'It is not good for the man to be alone' (Gen. 2:18), acknowledging that Adam was in an inferior condition without a mate. The need for each other and their deep sense of mutual dependence are what make marriage so satisfying," p. 25. In addition, God himself is portrayed like Eve, as a "helper" (Gen. 4:1, 49:25; Dt. 33.26).

(and commending their love and adoration as far exceeding that of those who claimed to be religious (Lk. 7:36–50; Matt. 26:6–13; Mk. 14:3–9; and Jn. 12:1–8). It contrasts both with the fact that women were treated in the early church as having equal religious status with men (Acts 1:14 and 12:12ff; and Romans 16 *passim*), and the uncompromising theological statements of the apostle Paul (Gal. 3:28).[111]

After reviewing all of the above arguments, thankfully the one rabbi that was a stripe of a different color was Jesus. Again Jesus understands the intention of the Father in creating the sexes in the first place (Matt. 19:7; Mk. 10:4); which is unity and union.[112]

When you begin to see the scope of women in the Bible who had legitimate callings and anointings, it begins to become undeniable that their place in the "Christian World," not to mention the culture in general, is one of equality and dignity. In Proverbs 8, wisdom is portrayed as a fearless woman standing in the middle of the city and crying out with a loud voice, "To you, O men, I call, and my cry is to the sons of men" (Prov. 8:4). She preaches authoritatively, and to men, evangelizing if you will in the central square of her city.

Negative attitudes toward women making any advancement in life or culture is so ingrained in our world that it can only be broken, in the author's opinion, by a "revelation" in the heart of man. It is time to put to rest the worldly patriarchal system of

---

[111] Summerton, *A Noble Task*, 136.
[112] "Throughout scripture the concept of *union* is the most important biblical theme relating to marriage. The uniqueness of holy matrimony is that a man and a woman can unite in a physical and spiritual harmony that supersedes that which can be achieved in any other human relationship. Marriage is not about who is in control or who serves whom. It is about *becoming one*. But a married couple cannot enjoy this deep level of oneness if the man views the woman as an inferior person," Grady, *10 Lies*, 26.

oppression of women that has bled into the church for centuries. It is time we release women to their rightful callings in the Lord.

Historical Foundation

As the original apostles began to die out, the "second generation" of leaders was waiting in the wings to move the church forward. The church was expanding northward, eastward, and southward rapidly. By the beginning of the second century, there seemed to be a general need to clarify the organization of church government. This we shall refer to as progressive ecclesiology.[113]

This paper will establish the idea that the above-mentioned clarification process relative to the ecclesiology of the newly burgeoning church became significantly altered due to cultural and theological factors; leaving the church with an attenuated leadership model wholly unrecognizable to that which was founded by the apostles. A brief survey of early Patristic history will establish this conclusion.

The reason for an adjustment to the ecclesiastical pattern set down by Paul, Peter, Timothy, and Titus seems to converge around four separate areas. First, Gnosticism[114] threatened to

---

[113] Perhaps the eschatology of the original apostles prevented them from institutionalizing the function of bishops, elders, and deacons for a subsequent church. We know that both Peter and Paul expected the imminent return of the Lord in their lifetime. However, those who followed them saw fit to make significant changes, perhaps needed, but wholly unrecognizable to the early church.

[114] "An early religious movement that believed that a specific *gnosis*, or 'knowledge,' could be obtained as a key to human salvation. With its roots in both Jewish theology and Greek philosophy, this movement gained a wide following among early Christians and became popular within Egyptian Christianity. Eventually, specific schools of Gnosticism and their teachers were rejected by the mainstream church as inconsistent with an orthodox Christian faith." Clayton N. Jefford, *Reading the Apostolic Fathers: A Students Introduction* (Grand Rapids, MI: Baker Academic, 2012), 183.

take over Christianity. Because of this, a certain pattern of leadership began to emerge around structure and authority[115] in an attempt to keep the locus of orthodoxy protected. Secondly, "persecution by the Roman government created a felt need for a strong central leadership to hold the church together."[116] F. F. Bruce reminds us that "two hundred years were to elapse before the Roman state accepted the presence of the church; before that time intermittent attempts were made to repress and, if possible, extirpate Christianity."[117] Thirdly, well into the second century, the books of the New Testament had been widely recognized and read: however, there was no official universal text to appeal to in the event of various disputes.[118] "Those churches which claimed an apostolic foundation attached great importance to the maintenance of the teaching which they had originally received."[119] Hence, a need for centralized leadership to intervene, so that theological issues could be addressed with credibility.

Finally, there was the issue of replacement theology (supersessionism), which states that Christianity has forever replaced Judaism as the one access to God, including the Christian church replacing Israel as the people of God. Similarly, Christians have forever replaced Jesus for Israel in the economy of salvation.[120] Because of the convergence of these four historical

---

[115] Jefford, *Reading the Apostolic Fathers*, 48.
[116] James Rutz, *MegaShift* (Colorado Springs, CO: Empowerment Press, 2005), 115.
[117] F. F. Bruce, *New Testament History* (Garden City, NY: Anchor Books, 1969), 415.
[118] Rutz, *MegaShift*, 215.
[119] Bruce, *New Testament*, 415.
[120] These definitions were taken from a lecture in Efrat, Israel, June 14, 2014, given by Dr. John Garr. For more information reference: johngarr@hebraiccenter.org

80 Biblical Eldership

"bumps in the road," the office of elder and bishop became attenuated so that the unfolding ecclesiology of the church became drastically altered, leaving a footprint that can still be seen in present-day Catholicism and much of Protestantism.[121]

Patristic Ecclesiology A.D. 100–400

The crucial period for ecclesiastical changes in the church came during the first 300 years. Let's look at a few of the major players. Our first subject is Clement of Rome, written between A.D. 95–96 with reference to persecution in Rome and associated with the ruler Domitian. Clement was one of the leaders and early bishops of the church in Rome and in our text is writing to a sister church in Corinth, out of concern that younger members had been successful in deposing some elder men of the hierarchy without due process.[122] When in reading the account, one is left

---

[121] Ronald Diprose, speaking of the New Testament church, gives us an insightful paragraph at this point: "The most important ministries envisaged for church leaders were teaching and pastoral care (Acts 20:28-31; 1 Peter 5:1-4), while deacons were responsible to meet the practical needs of the congregation. However, the concept of ministry was not limited to the roles of bishops and deacons. Both Peter and Paul conceive of the Church as a society in which every member has his or her function and is called to serve according to the particular *charisma* ('gift of grace') received (1 Peter 4:10-11; Romans 12:4-8; 1 Corinthians 12:7-30). In light of later developments, it is striking that nowhere in the New Testament are elders invested with a priestly function which sets them apart from the rest of the church. Moreover, no list of spiritual gifts includes a particular *charisma* for performing priestly functions. The purpose of all the gifts was the edification of the church, not mediation between God and other church members." Ronald E. Diprose, *Israel and the Church: The Origin and Effects of Replacement Theology* (Rome, Italy: Istituto Biblico Evangelico Italiano, 2004), 102.

[122] George A. Buttrick, ed., *A-D*, vol. 1, *The Interpreter's Dictionary of the Bible* (Nashville, TN: Abingdon Press, 1962), 648.

with the impression that these older elders were legitimately appointed presbyters and should not have been dismissed out of hand. Clement is concerned not only with a breach of integrity, but also with its result affecting the whole church. He writes: "Why are there strife, and tumults, and divisions, and schisms, and wars among you? Why do we divide and tear to pieces the members of Christ?"[123] As we look a little further in the discourse, we see the real motivation for his reprimand: "Let him who has love in Christ keep the commandments of Christ. There is nothing base, nothing arrogant in love. Love admits of no schisms: love gives rise to no seditions: love does all things in harmony."[124] Things seem to be very close to the original ecclesiology of the Apostles. However, this changes quickly within a decade or so. Ignatius gives us our first glimpse.

Ignatius, Bishop of Antioch (A.D. 98–117)[125], has some

---

[123] Clement of Rome, "The First Epistle of Clement to the Corinthians," in *The Apostolic Fathers with Justin Martyr and Irenaeus*, vol. 1, *The Ante-Nicene Fathers*, A. Roberts, J. Donaldson, and A. C. Coxe, eds. (Buffalo, NY: Christian Literature Company, 1885), 17–18, Logos Bible Software. Clement continues, "It is disgraceful, beloved, yea, highly disgraceful, and unworthy of your Christian profession, that such a thing should be heard of as that the most steadfast and ancient Church of the Corinthians should, on account of one or two persons, engage in sedition against its presbyters. And this rumor has reached not only us, but those also who are unconnected with us; so that, through your infatuation, the name of the Lord is blasphemed, while danger is also brought upon yourselves" (chapter 47). It seems that Clement is very concerned that the matrix of the structure given by the Apostles should not be abbreviated.

[124] *Ante-Nicene Fathers*, 1:chapter 49.

[125] "Ignatius was on his way to martyrdom in Rome in Trajan's reign, when he wrote seven letters which were gathered into a corpus: to the Asian churches at Ephesus, Magnesia, Tralles, Philadelphia and Smyrna, to his friend Polycarp, bishop of Smyrna, and to the Roman church, asking them not to intervene to prevent his martyrdom." *Ante-Nicene Fathers*, 1:879.

insightful words concerning his understanding of progressive ecclesiology. To the Magnesians he writes: "As therefore the Lord did nothing without the Father, being united to Him, neither by Himself nor by the apostles, so neither do ye anything without the bishop and presbyters."[126] In a section on preserving honor, to the same group, he writes: "Your bishop presides in the place of God, and your presbyters in the place of the assembly of the apostles, along with your deacons, who are most dear to me, and are entrusted with the ministry of Jesus Christ."[127] In his letter to the Trallians, he writes, "In like manner, let all reverence the deacons as an appointment of Jesus Christ, and the bishop as Jesus Christ, who is the Son of the Father, and the presbyters as the Sanhedrin of God, and assembly of the apostles."[128] Continuing on, his letter to the Philadelphians states: "Take ye heed, then, to have but one Eucharist. For there is one flesh of our Lord Jesus Christ, and one cup to [show forth] the unity of His blood; one altar; as there is one bishop, along with the presbytery and deacons, my fellow-servants: that so, whatsoever ye do, ye do it according to the will of God."[129]

And finally to the Smyraeans, he writes: "It is not lawful without the bishop either to baptize or to celebrate a love-feast . . . ."[130] Clifford Jefford makes the observation that Ignatius "was anxious that the structure of authority within the early church

---

[126] Ignatius of Antioch, "The Epistle of Ignatius to the Magnesians," in *The Apostolic Fathers with Justin Martyr and Irenaeus*, vol. 1, *The Ante-Nicene Fathers*, A. Roberts, J. Donaldson, and A. C. Coxe, eds. (Buffalo, NY: Christian Literature Company, 1885), 61-62, Logos Bible Software.
[127] *Ante-Nicene Fathers*, 1:62.
[128] *Ante-Nicene Fathers*, 1:67.
[129] *Ante-Nicene Fathers*, 1:81.
[130] *Ante-Nicene Fathers*, 1:89–90. In the same context, he also makes this statement to Polycarp's church at Smyrna: "Wherever the bishop shall appear, there let the multitude [of the people] also be; even as, wherever Jesus Christ is, there is the Catholic Church."

develop according to a certain pattern."[131] Unfortunately the pattern included a defined hierarchy with what others have termed the *monarchial bishop*.[132] F. F. Bruce weighs in on this early development called the monarchial episcopate. He says the monarchical bishop was "one bishop in control of the administration of the church of a city—replacing the earlier government of each church by a body of elders or bishops."[133]

The Second Century A.D.

We now turn our attention to another giant among those who followed the Apostles. I am speaking of Polycarp, bishop of Smyrna (A.D. 69–155). Polycarp had a very long and full life. He is referred to by both Irenaeus and Eusebius as having known and having been instructed by the Apostle John and many others who had seen Christ.[134] Polycarp wrote a letter to the church in Philippi, having been grieved over some financial misdealings of one of the elders named Valens, and his wife. He says in Chapter

---

[131] Jefford, *Reading the Apostolic Fathers*, 48.

[132] Dr. Kenneth Collins, professor of historical theology and Wesley studies at Asbury Theological Seminary, comments on this development in second-century Christians with reference to Catholicism when he says, "Though the first-century church knew nothing of a monarchical bishop (the bishop 'above' the elder), the preeminence of Rome, or a pope for that matter (many historians consider Leo I of the fifth century or Gregory I of the sixth to be the first pope), these developments in *polity* are nonetheless legitimized by an appeal to tradition, given virtually equal weight with the teaching of Scripture, and are thereby required to be affirmed by all the faithful." Kenneth J. Collins, *The Evangelical Moment: The Promise of an American Religion* (Grand Rapids, MI: Baker Academic, 2005), 186.

[133] Bruce, *New Testament*, 4.

[134] "Introductory Note to the Epistle of Polycarp to the Philippians," in *The Apostolic Fathers with Justin Martyr and Irenaeus*, vol. 1, *The Ante-Nicene Fathers*, A. Roberts, J. Donaldson, and A. C. Coxe, eds. (Buffalo, NY: Christian Literature Company, 1885), 31-32, Logos Bible Software.

84   Biblical Eldership

VI, "I am greatly grieved for Valens, who was over a presbytery among you, because he so little understands the place that was given him in the church.[135] I am deeply grieved, therefore, brethren, for him and his wife; to whom may the Lord grant repentance."[136] Note the use of the article in "a presbyter" (singular), not the presbyter. In fact he begins his letter with these words: "Polycarp, and the presbyters with him, to the church of God sojourning at Philippi; Mercy to you, and peace from God Almighty, and from the Lord Jesus Christ, our Savior, be multiplied."[137] Obviously Polycarp is himself involved in a plurality of leadership and recognizes that the church at Philippi is as well. This is confirmed by the Apostle Paul's opening statement to the Philippians in the New Testament (Phil. 1:1). So as far as Polycarp is concerned, the notion of the monarchial bishop had not yet taken hold.[138]

One last note on Polycarp: he was burned at the stake, on February 1, 185 (Eusebius, Hist. IV.15), after having been encouraged to deny his Lord.[139] He told the crowd, "Eighty-six years have I served him, and He has done me no wrong; how can I blaspheme my Savior and King?"[140]

---

[135] *Ante-Nicene Fathers*, 1:chapter 6.
[136] *Ante-Nicene Fathers*, 1:chapter 11.
[137] *Ante-Nicene Fathers*, 1:31-32.
[138] It is helpful to remember as Darrell Guder reminds us: "The Christian church of the second century developed in a social and political world shaped by monarchy and centralized hierarchical power. It is no wonder that the monarchical bishop emerged as the most authoritative figure within the church. The papal office followed the cultural track laid out by the Roman emperor, assuming even his title 'Pontifex.'" Darrell L. Guder, ed., *Missional Church: A Vision for the Sending of the Church in North America* (Grand Rapids, MI: William B. Eerdmans Publishing Co., 1998), 232.
[139] George A. Buttrick, ed., *K-Q*, vol. 3, *The Interpreter's Dictionary of the Bible* (Nashville, TN: Abingdon Press, 1962), 840.
[140] F. F. Bruce, *The Spreading Flame: The Rise and Progress of Christianity*

Theoretical Foundation 85

Our next example is Tertullian, Bishop of Carthage (A.D. 160–225). He was without a doubt the "most important and eloquent theologian in the West at the end of the second century."[141] "As a brilliant polemical writer, he was the earliest writer of Christian Latin, and represented the 'Latin Tradition.'"[142] "He coined terminology which was to dominate Western theology—for example, *trinitas,* 'three persons in one substance,' or of Christ, 'two substances or natures in one person.'"[143] However, when it came to ecclesiology, he was in lockstep with most all the ancient divines. Congregations were led by bishops, elders, and deacons. James Rutz gives us a telling sentence on Tertullian's concept of order in the church: "It is the authority of the church, and the honor which has acquired sanctity through the joint session of the Order, which has established the difference between the Order and the laity."[144] In other words, "in the matter of dividing the church into clergy and laity, we're making this up as we go along. We are now our own authority."[145] All this can be further seen in a statement that the bishop made on baptism.[146] It is fair

---

from its First Beginnings to the Conversion of the English (Grand Rapids, MI: Wm. B. Eerdmans Publishing Co., 1958), 174.
[141] John McManners, ed., *The Oxford Illustrated History of Christianity* (New York: Oxford University Press, 1992), 48.
[142] Steven Gertz, "Opponents of Allegory," *Christian History* 42, no. 4 (2003): 27.
[143] *Oxford Illustrated*, 50.
[144] Rutz, *MegaShift*, 219.
[145] Rutz, *MegaShift*, 220.
[146] "For concluding our brief subject, it remains to put you in mind also of the due observance of giving and receiving baptism. Of giving it, the chief priest (who is the bishop) has the right: in the next place, the presbyters and deacons, yet not without the bishop's authority, on account of the honor of the Church, which being preserved, peace is preserved." Tertullian, "On Baptism," in *Latin Christianity: Its Founder, Tertullian,* vol. 3, *The Ante-Nicene Fathers,* A. Roberts, J. Donaldson, and

to say that, late in his journey, Tertullian joined the Montanists;[147] he began to back away from the accepted ecclesiology of the Catholic hierarchy. In the spirit of a more charismatic understanding of the church, "he could argue that there can be no difference between clergy and laity, since authority belongs to those who possess the Spirit and not to bishops as such."[148] Tertullian's attempt to re-emphasize the Spirit's authority over against the church hierarchy did not carry the day.

In this same period of time, another great figure of the Alexandrian tradition was Origen of Alexandria (A.D. 185–254). Truly one of the greatest minds of the early patristic era, Origen was the eldest of seven children. He grew up in a Christian home with intentional Bible learning. As a result, he was well schooled in the faith through precept and example. In fact, his father, Leonids, was beheaded for his Christian beliefs in the year A.D. 202.[149] Origen wanted to follow his father into martyrdom, but his mother prevented him from doing so, by hiding his clothes.[150] He couldn't leave the house!

A. C. Coxe, eds. (Buffalo, NY: Christian Literature Company, 1885), chapter 17, Logos Bible Software. He did go on to say that in the event that the hierarchy was not available, that baptism was "equally God's property" and could be administered by laymen as well.

[147] Jefford, *Reading the Apostolic Fathers*, 185. Dr. Jefford defines Montanism as: "An early Christian prophetic movement that was prevalent in Asia Minor during the late second through fourth centuries AD. The movement was named after the ecstatic prophet Montanus (ca. 170), who insisted that a true prophet could not be restricted by the rational mind. He was eventually excommunicated by Eleutherus, bishop of Rome, in the year 177."

[148] J. N. D. Kelly, *Early Christian Doctrines* (New York: Harper Collins Publishers, Revised Edition, 1978), 200.

[149] John R. Franke, "Origen: Friend or Foe?," *Christian History* 22, no. 4 (2003): 19.

[150] Franke, "Origen," 19.

Pursuing a first-rate education in one of the greatest intellectual centers in the ancient world (Alexandria), his dual competency in both Hellenistic and Christian disciplines "could have caused an internal tension in Origen, as he sought to reconcile his commitment to Christian faith and the Bible, with the classic teachings of ancient Greece."[151] Following his father's demise, he became the leading teacher in a well-known school of Christian catechism. This experience afforded Origen a perfect environment to exercise his astute intellectual skills. Here, he was able to write freely because there was very little persecution of Christians until the middle of the third century in Alexandria.[152]

A patron and friend of Origen was generous and provided him with a cohort of scribes (copyists, stenographers, and calligraphers) so as to accelerate his work.[153] His dominant method of scriptural interpretation was allegorical, making his logic available to a broad spectrum of people schooled in Greek thought, and his method of interpretation actually became the dominant method used in a deeper understanding of the scriptures all the way through the Middle Ages.[154]

On a ministry visit to Caesarea in Palestine, he was ordained a presbyter in the church of that area by the hierarchy who had asked him to come and speak.[155] His election to presbyter became an experience that caused him more than a little trouble through the years. When his home bishop Demetrius heard of the incident, he was mortified. The following year in A.D. 231,

---

[151] Franke, "Origen," 18.
[152] Charles Freeman, *A New History of Early Christianity* (New Haven, CT.: Yale University Press, 2009), 187.
[153] Franke, "Origen," 19.
[154] Franke, "Origen," 20.
[155] Origen accepted the emerging hierarchy of the Catholic Church, though he never actually sought a position himself.

Demetrius summoned a synod "composed of Egyptian bishops and Alexandrian presbyters, who declared Origen unworthy to hold the office of teacher, and excommunicated him from the fellowship of the church in Alexandria."[156] Following this unpleasant experience, Origen moved to Caesarea, a town where he spent the last twenty-five years of his life, while mostly avoiding persecution and developing a very impressive library.[157]

His friend Ambrose persuaded Origen to refute a major assault on Christianity by a man named Celsus. So Origen wrote a treatise entitled *Against Celsus*, which became a defense of Christian faith "against the critique of the Roman philosopher Celsus, in which Origen attempted to demonstrate the superiority of the teachings of the Bible versus Greek philosophy."[158] In chapter twenty-five of the defense, he seems to undergird the ecclesiology of the Roman See.[159] Along with the Apologies of Justin and Tertullian, Origen's *Contra Celsus* establishes the fact that the early church could refute any and all

---

[156] "Introductory Note to the Works of Origen," in *Fathers of the Third Century: Tertullian, Part Fourth; Minucius Felix; Commodian; Origen, Parts First and Second*, vol. 4, *The Ante-Nicene Fathers*, A. Roberts, J. Donaldson, and A. C. Coxe, eds. (Buffalo, NY: Christian Literature Company, 1885), 227, Logos Bible Software.
[157] *Ante-Nicene Fathers*, 4:227.
[158] Franke, "Origen," 20.
[159] He says, "Celsus also urges us to take office in the government of the country, if that is required for the maintenance of the laws and the support of religion. But we recognize in each state the existence of another national organization, founded by the Word of God, and we exhort those who are mighty in word and of blameless life to rule over churches. Those who are ambitious or ruling we reject; but we constrain those who, through excess of modesty, are not easily induced to take a public charge in the church of God." "Origen against Celsus," trans. F. Crombie, in *Fathers of the Third Century: Tertullian, Part Fourth; Minucius Felix; Commodian; Origen, Parts First and Second*, vol. 4, *The Ante-Nicene Fathers*, A. Roberts, J. Donaldson, and A. C. Coxe, eds. (Buffalo, NY: Christian Literature Company, 1885), chapter 75, Logos Bible Software.

Hellenistic theological derivatives.[160] However, his digression from orthodox belief concerning "eternal hell" caused him to be labeled a heretic three centuries after his death, at the Council of Constantinople in A.D. 553, with the searing phrase, "whosoever says or thinks that the punishment of demons and the wicked will not be eternal—let him be anathema."[161]

The Reformation and Progressive Ecclesiology

"On October 31, 1517 Martin Luther, Professor of Biblical Studies at the University of Wittenberg, Saxony, posted a set of ninety-five theological propositions, or 'theses,' dealing with the church practice of indulgences."[162] This simple act resulted in a firestorm of controversy within the Catholic Church and ultimately birthed the Protestant Reformation.[163] Within this matrix of upheaval, Luther's argument was not so much with the ecclesiastical structure[164] of the church as with its inane theology and corrupt procedures with respect to the selling of indulgences (a kind of pass enabling people to avoid purgatory, even though their

---

[160] Charles Freeman, *A New History of Early Christianity* (New Haven, CT.: Yale University Press, 2009), 194.

[161] Mark Galli and Ted Olsen, eds., *131 Christians Everyone Should Know* (Nashville, TN: Broadman and Holman Publishers, 2000), 334.

[162] Hillerbrand, *A New History of Christianity* (Nashville: Abingdon Press, 2012), 147.

[163] "The situation of Christendom in the year 1500, two decades before Martin Luther began the Reformation, was dreadful. The church in the New Testament was persecuted and politically powerless, but filled with the miracle working power of the Spirit, and its congregations often practiced the gifts of the Spirit. The Church of the year 1500 persecuted dissent and any form of 'irregular ideas' with torture and execution, exercised great political power, but was largely empty of the gifts, presence and power of the Spirit." William De Artega, *Forging a Renewed Hebraic and Pauline Christianity* (not yet published), 75.

[164] The church of Luther's day was organized much as it is even today with bishops, archbishops, and cardinals.

actions and lifestyle deserved it). Luther's main problem with the structure of the church centered on "the question of church authority and its sacramental system."[165]

Since the church was totally dominated by professional clergy, any role of the laymen or elders remained nonexistent. When pressed to defend his ninety-five theses at a debate arranged by the Catholic hierarchy in June of 1519 in the city of Leipzig, he actually "denied the ultimate authority of the church (and of church councils) in favor of the authority of scripture, a stance that evoked gasps of dismay from the faithful Catholics and sharpened the gulf between the Wittenberg friar and his church."[166] Through a circuitous route of events, Martin Luther was excommunicated from the church as a heretic, and with this his fate was clear: "The political authorities would apprehend him and condemn him in a perfunctory trial to death by burning, the punishment reserved for heretics, whose bodies and souls were reduced to ashes."[167] The Edict of Worms made Luther a legal outlaw, and he went into hiding until his death in 1546.

John Calvin (1509-1564)

John Calvin, born in France and raised in the Catholic Church, was a bright scholar who held much potential for a promising career. As a young Frenchman, following the behest of his father, Calvin began the study of law arriving in Orleans, "the ancient city named for the Roman Emperor Marcus Aurelius, 80 miles south of Paris."[168] In Orleans, he studied under a long-recognized outstanding French jurist by the name of Pierre de L'Estoile, who

---

[165] Hillerbrand, *New History*, 153.
[166] Hillerbrand, *New History*, 147.
[167] Hillerbrand, *New History*, 158.
[168] Bruce Gordon, *Calvin* (New Haven, CT: Yale University Press, 2009), 19.

was also the vicar-general of the diocese of Orleans.[169] In this stead, Calvin was "exposed to the complex interrelationship of legal studies, the church and politics."[170] However, in 1533, Calvin

> Experienced a sudden conversion [w]hich subdued and brought my mind to a teachable frame, which was more hardened in such matters than might have been expected from one at my early period of life. Having thus received some taste and knowledge of true godliness I was immediately inflamed with so intense a desire to make progress therein, that although I did not altogether leave off other studies, I yet pursued them with less ardour.[171]

As Calvin was drawn deeper into the rudiments of the Protestant Reformation, his ecclesiology became clearly defined. In 1541 "the Geneva city council solicited Calvin to return to Geneva,[172] as head of the Geneva Church. He agreed with one condition: the promulgation of a new church order for the Geneva Church."[173] With this caveat[174] we see Calvin lay out what would become distinctive in Protestant theology with respect to ecclesiology, the four congregational offices of pastor, teacher, elder, and deacon.[175] By this model Calvin asserted that:

> Pastors preached and administered the sacraments, teachers

---

[169] Gordon, *Calvin*, 19.
[170] Gordon, *Calvin*, 19.
[171] Gordon, *Calvin*, 33.
[172] Calvin had been to Geneva previously through the influence of his good friend Guillaume Farel, but left the city on unfriendly terms.
[173] Hillerbrand, *New History*, 178.
[174] Calvin was dealing with issues relative to the Papacy, and as Bruce Gordon has noted the issue that "the pope had risen to such an eminence, certainly not appointed head of the church by the Word of God, nor ordained by a legitimate act of the church, but of his own accord." Gordon, *Calvin,* 33–34.
[175] Hillerbrand, *New History*, 179.

expounded Scripture, elders[176] (in Latin, "presbyters") had overall responsibility for the life of the congregation, while deacons cared for the physical needs of its members. Calvin determinedly set out to organize the Genevan church—and indeed all congregations he influenced—in accord with this model.[177]

"Within the remarkably brief period of two months Calvin succeeded in having the framework of a new church order drawn up and passed by the Geneva council."[178] What became known as the "Ecclesiastical Ordinances" became official law on November 20, 1541, and this framework "expressed Calvin's understanding of the church as developed in the 1539 *Institutes*, in his commentary on Romans, and in his experiences of working as a minister in Strasbourg."[179] Many aspects of this framework continue to exist today in the Protestant sector of the church known as "Reformed theology."

John Wesley and the Methodists

The flowering of the laity in church government and ecclesiology came under the greatest figure of the First Great Awakening, John Wesley. Mr. Wesley developed a defined and effective

---

[176] "The clarity and simplicity of Calvin's understanding of the Christian faith were widely found compelling and attractive, and they help explain the appeal of Calvinism throughout Europe, especially in Scotland which formally turned Protestant in 1560. But even more important, Calvin's notions of the organization of local congregations afforded laypersons (as "elders" or "presbyters") the opportunity to be active leaders in running the affairs of the congregation. Calvinism, in other words, presented itself as the religion of the new type of individual in Europe: the self-confident layman, the lower nobility, the gentry. In Calvinist congregations, the laypersons had the opportunity to play an enormously important role." Hillerbrand, *New History*, 180.
[177] Hillerbrand, *New History*, 179.
[178] Gordon, *Calvin*, 126.
[179] Gordon, *Calvin*, 126.

protocol for tracking individuals who were serious about their journey of growth in Christ. The beauty of the Methodist system was that people could remain in their denomination of allegiance and still participate in the revival. Even Wesley himself did this.[180] Adherents were encouraged to take the sacraments in their home church while they engaged in discipleship meetings during the week with the Methodists.

Wesley's issue with the Anglican Church "was not doctrinal, for John faithfully accepted the teachings of the Anglican Church. At issue was the insistence on a committed Christian life and the concern for the lower classes of English society, whom the church had come to neglect."[181] The genius of the eighteenth-century revival under Wesley was an elaborate organizational design for discipleship. Methodist theology was missional as well as propositional. In modern terms, you can't just show people pictures of the Grand Canyon; you have to take them there to actually experience it. This is what Wesley did through his network. In addition, most of the people recruited for leadership in his network were laymen, not ordained clergy. Wesley and Calvin would have been on the same page at this point. Even today, "lay preachers" are an important part of the UMC in America.

The Methodist movement was organized around three basic clusters of people: societies, classes, and bands. Societies were the largest of the three groupings and were basically geographical in

---

[180] Mr. Wesley, referring to this concept in a treatise called "The Ministerial Office" just two years before he died, makes the following statement: "With the Methodists it is quite otherwise: They are not a sect or party; they do not separate from the religious community to which they at first belonged; they are still members of the Church—such they desire to live and to die. And I believe one reason why God is pleased to continue my life so long is, to confirm them in their present purpose, not to separate from the Church." Wesley, *Works*, 3:278.
[181] Hillerbrand, *New History*, 236.

94 Biblical Eldership

nature. In the society any number of people could associate together to pursue holiness and love for God. Their membership in a society in most cases followed their conversion experience. The vortex of their association was plain to everyone: "They wanted to flee from the wrath to come, and to assist each other in so doing. They would pray together, to receive the word of exhortation, and to watch over one another in love, that they might help each other to work out their salvation."[182]

To better care for these "seekers," Wesley broke them down into "class meetings" of approximately twelve persons. Each class would have a leader (a layman) appointed to gather the group once a week for the purpose of examining "how their souls prosper, to advise, reprove, confront, or exhort, as occasion may require; to receive what they are willing to give, toward the relief of the poor."[183] For those who were even more diligent and displayed progress to go deeper in their Christian walk, Wesley organized "bands"[184]—"putting the married and single men, and married and single women together."[185] In this construct, they would "study, pray, confess their faults to one another, sing, confess their sins, and reveal the temptations and longings of their souls."[186] The bands also meet personally once a week with

---

[182] Wesley, *Works*, 8:250.
[183] Wesley, *Works*, 8:253.
[184] In the bands, the "aim originally had been to promote the cultivation of the soul and the development of the inner life. The design was to afford a place which would separate those who wanted to become deeply religious and to move toward Christian perfection from those who were content to be morally upright and respectable. The band offered a graduate course in piety, and members were to be chosen from the more earnest and serious members of the classes, those most acquainted with each other and able to discuss each other's souls in intimacy and candor." Charles W. Ferguson, *Organizing to Beat the Devil: Methodists and the Making of America* (Garden City, NY: Doubleday & Company Inc., 1971), 74.
[185] Ferguson, *Organizing to Beat*, 258.
[186] Ferguson, *Organizing to Beat*, 258.

Mr. Wesley, and once a quarter they met in a combined meeting with both men and women. There, as Mr. Wesley describes, they would "eat bread as the ancient Christians did, with gladness and singleness of heart. At these love-feasts (so we termed them, retaining the name, as well as the thing, which was in use from the beginning) our food is only a little plain cake and water. But we seldom return from them without being fed, not only with the 'meat which perisheth,' but with 'that which endureth to everlasting life.'"[187] Finally, in order to properly supervise all these meetings, Wesley appointed "leaders of classes, bands, assistants, Stewards, visitors of the sick and School masters."[188] Most all of this leadership was lay driven.

With the inception of these various spiritual life groups, the Methodist movement could be very large in scope; but also small and manageable. Through open-air preaching[189], Wesley appealed to the masses for converts and that with amazing results; however, it was the small-cell grouping that became the genius of the movement, because suddenly there was a need for follow-up with these new creatures of the Kingdom of God. The Methodists have been left a rich legacy of lay preachers who

---

[187] Ferguson, *Organizing to Beat*, 259.
[188] Ferguson, *Organizing to Beat*, 261.
[189] In the beginning of his field preaching, John Wesley was clearly out of his comfort zone, but into his anointing. With it he crossed over a historical threshold that set into motion the entire Wesleyan Revival, by calling the common man to Christ in the open-air stage. A portion of his journal tells the whole story: "Thursday, March 29th 1739: 'In the evening I reached Bristol, and met Mr. Whitefield there. I could scarce reconcile myself at first to this strange way of preaching in the fields, of which he set me an example on Sunday; having been all my life (till very lately) so tenacious of every point relating to decency and order, that I should have thought the saving of souls almost a sin, if it had not been done in a church.'" Wesley continues with a revealing entry on Monday April 2, 1739: "At four in the afternoon, I submitted to be more vile, and proclaimed in the highways the glad tiding of salvation, speaking from a little eminence in a ground adjoining to the city to about three thousand people." Wesley, *Works*, 1:185.

actually became a form of *presbyter* after the pattern of the New Testament. The Methodist heritage holds promise for many in the contemporary church of the twenty-first century to go on with God and reform the land through scriptural holiness.[190] With a moderate amount of tweaking, Wesley's pattern could be fully employed in the church today.

Conclusion

With hindsight at our disposal, it is easy to look back and see where the church took a fork in the road and perhaps made unfortunate decisions concerning its structure and ministry. When determining authority for our actions, we must first and foremost turn to scripture. As Thomas and Wondra have said in their recent book on theology, "The essential difference between canonical and extracanonical writings is that canonical writings constitute the first written deposit of the original testimony to God's revelation, whereas extracanonical writings are dependent on this testimony."[191] And furthermore, "the church knew intuitively which writings it wanted in the canon, that is, which writings bore the clearest and fullest testimony to Christ, produced authentic Christian conversion, Christian life, and the

---

[190] Wesley went forward in the open-air venue because he was conquered by a truth that was greater than his fear. The new converts hardly realized that they were beginning a journey to crucify the flesh and strangle sin at its root. The perennial problem of sin was always near in eighteenth- and nineteenth-century England. In one of the most well-known stories of English literature, *The Adventures of Sherlock Holmes*, the detective Holmes says to his counterpart: "It is my belief, Watson, founded on my experience, that the lowest and vilest alleys of large cities do not present a more dreadful record of sin than does the smiling and beautiful country side." Arthur Conan Doyle, *The Complete Sherlock Holmes* (New York: Barnes and Noble Signature Edition, Sterling Publishing Inc., 2012), 1:374.

[191] Owen C. Thomas and Ellen K. Wondra, *Introduction to Theology*, 3rd ed. (New York: Morehouse Publishing, 2002), 54.

fruit of the Spirit, the 'demonstration of the Spirit and power (I Cor. 2:4).'"[192] Dr. Kenneth Collins from Asbury Seminary weighs in on this thought in his book *The Evangelical Moment* when he says, "Scripture as the Word of God holds primacy among secondary elements employed by the church to preserve the substance and integrity of the *kerygma*."[193] Therefore we should as well receive the testimony from the New Testament as authoritative when determining God's favor toward any original pattern of faith and ministry.

Since the history of Christian ecclesiology suggests a migration of concepts and sacerdotal arrangements through the centuries, most of which were significantly altered from the New Testament pattern, one could envision a further migration back to the original pattern of the Apostles—a kind of "back to the future," and with it a new ecclesiological design for the church of the twenty-first century. As we continue, I argue for such a design in the twenty-first century church.

Theological Foundation

The theological foundations section of this paper continues to reference an area of church administration known as ecclesiology[194] including specific reference to the Reformation doctrine of the Priesthood of the Believer over against the present Western denominational concept of pastor/teacher and its implications for local church effectiveness and health in the twenty-first century. With the author's presuppositions on display and his theological bias at hand, he will argue for a leadership model available to most any congregation eschewing disruption to its existent structure.

---

[192] Thomas and Wondra, *Introduction*, 55.
[193] Collins, *Evangelical Moment*, 193.
[194] "The Science of Church Organization and Management," in *Webster's New Universal Unabridged Dictionary*, 2nd ed, s.v. "ecclesiology."

A simple New Testament structure known as Biblical Eldership,[195] when Holy Spirit-grounded and charismatically gifted, will elevate and enhance the ministry function of pastor/teacher in its local setting beyond any traditional ecclesiastical matrix.[196] In other words, this paper continues to maintain that the breadth and depth of pastoral administration is enhanced when elders are set in place in the local church.

Western Christianity has piled on century after century of a deleterious leadership pattern composed of three designations—bishop, elder, and deacon—as the primary ecclesiastical template for local church administration. Within this trinity of oversight,

---

[195] "In the New Testament, the Christian eldership is established, and the Jewish-Christian institution of eldership helps to unify the diversities of NT ministry, more than is often realized. Inherited from an Old Testament design, the NT elder takes their cause from Christ, the one great teacher or rabbi (Matt. 23:8). His disciples call themselves elders (1 Peter 5:1; 2 John 1:3). They pass on the teaching they have received and commit it to others, who are to commit it to others again (1 Cor. 11:23, 15:1, 3; 2 Thess. 2:15, 3:6; 2 Thess. 2:2). Those to whom it is committed are likewise elders (Acts 14:23; Titus 1:5). They are apparently appointed by the laying on of hands (Acts 6:6; 1 Tim 4:14, 5:22; 2 Tim. 1:6). In addition to the tasks of teaching and judging, the task of ruling is reemphasized in Christian eldership, and gives a pastoral rather than a political character (Acts 20:17, 28: 1 Tim. 5:17; James 5:14; 1 Peter 5:1-4). The Christian eldership is primarily an office of teaching, of adjudicating questions of right and wrong, and of providing pastoral oversight." R.T. Beckwith, *New Bible Dictionary*, 2nd ed., editors: J. D. Douglas, F. F. Bruce, J. I. Packer, N. Hillyer, D. Guthrie, A. R. Millard, D. J. Wiseman (IVP, Downers Grove, IL, 1996), 965.

[196] Hans von Campenhausen begins his excellent book, *Ecclesiastical Authority and Spiritual Power in the Church of the First Three Centuries*, with the following insight: "In every culture and in all ages human society has known the tension between the position assigned to a man and the ability which the man's own inner resources allow him to display. The former endues all that he does with the force of law and of the commission which stands behind him; the latter bestows on him as a person immediate credibility, and is the convincing justification of his claims." Hans von Campenhausen, *Ecclesiastical Authority and Spiritual Power in the Church of the First Three Centuries* (Peabody, MA: Hendrickson Publishers Inc., 1997), 1. This tension in leadership is on display throughout this paper.

the pastor has been isolated as a know-all, end-all jack of all trades point person, resulting in the average church's orthopraxis becoming unrecognizable from the New Testament design of local church leadership. As a result, the Western concept of local church leadership has caused much angst[197] in the overall effectiveness of traditional Christianity in America.

In an attempt to bring us back on course, this study incorporates a pensive look at three areas of church ecclesiology: 1) the biblical concept of the Priesthood of the Believer, transvaluated by Martin Luther and John Calvin in the sixteenth century, versus a current, traditional, denominational ecclesiastical structure in ministry, known as bishop, elder, and deacon; 2) biblical authority in leadership mitigated by the New Testament *charismata* in a communal setting versus traditional ordination orders; and 3) a supernatural ministry construct versus a cultural construct utilizing sociological factors such as reason, program, resources, methodologies, demographics, finances, attendance patterns, and more to accentuate ministry effectiveness.

The Biblical Concept of the Priesthood of the Believer versus Traditional Denominational Structure

Today most mainline denominations,[198] along with many

---

[197] George Barna states that 80 percent of the churches in America have either plateaued or are in decline. As cited in Russell Burrill, "Can Dying Churches be Resuscitated?," *Ministry: International Journal for Pastors*, December 2002, 14.

[198] "Despite its common usage, 'mainline' is a difficult word to pin down. Scholarship on the Protestant mainline typically defines the term with reference to a set of denominations. The standard list—sometimes called the 'Seven Sisters'—includes the Episcopal Church, the Presbyterian Church (USA), the Northern Baptist Church, the Congregational Church (now part of the United Church of Christ), the United Methodist Church, the Evangelical Lutheran Church and the

nondenominational churches, embrace some form of a traditional ecclesiastical structure in ministry known as bishop, elder, and deacon.[199] Specifically, with respect to the office of elder, the contemporary church locates it in New Testament language but interprets it in a third-century historical understanding. For instance, the UMC adheres to the traditional three-part division of bishop, elder, and deacon; yet one may observe in *The Book of Discipline*[200] under the section titled, "Clergy Orders in the United Methodist Church," that paragraph 305 states: "Within the people of God, other persons are called to the ministry of elder. The elders carry on the historic work of the *presbyteros* in the life of the church."[201]

Disciples of Christ." Elesha J. Coffman, *The Christian Century and the Rise of the Protestant Mainline* (New York: Oxford University Press, 2013), 4. Ms. Coffman goes on to say concerning the term "mainline": "It suddenly emerged as a religious description right around 1960. Like most labels, it was bestowed by outsiders and was not readily accepted by those it described." (p. 213)

[199] "Although the pinnacle of what Martin Luther called the priesthood of all believers dates back to the sixteenth century, most churches still maintain a rigid demarcation between clergy and laity, and they concentrate most of the ministry in the hands of ordained leadership." Henry I. Lederle, *Theology with Spirit* (Tulsa, OK: Word and Spirit Press, 2012), 139. In addition, Darrell L. Guder reinforces Lederle's thought on the demarcation between clergy and laity with this incisive thought on clergy as professionals: "This view effectively eclipses the gifts for leadership in the non-ordained contingent of God's sent people, those known in Christendom as the laity. Ministry remains identified with the static roles of clergy as priest, pedagogue, or professional, all dispensers of spiritual resources. Even where the priesthood of all believers stands as a theological conviction of an ecclesiastical community, it is rarely practiced in the church." Darrell L. Guder, ed., *Missional Church: A Vision for the Sending of the Church in North America* (Grand Rapids, MI: William B. Eerdmans Publishing Co., 1998), 195.

[200] *BOD*.

[201] However, in delineating this order of ministry, they seem to assume a second- or third-century construct, not found in the New Testament.

Continuing in a section entitled "Candidacy for Licensed and Ordained Ministry," paragraph 310 states: "The licensed or ordained ministry is recognized by the United Methodist Church as a called-out and set-apart ministry."[202] In this vein, these persons so present themselves to be "examined regarding the authenticity of their call by God to ordained ministry."[203] This examination, of course, is conducted by church hierarchy, not by a local church, which was the New Testament pattern. Providing the candidate successfully passes all examinations and educational requirements, an elder shall be "ordained by a Bishop by the laying on of hands, employing the Order of Service for the Ordination of Elders."[204]

With this ordination fully in place, "Elders are ordained to a life time of ministry in Word, Sacrament, Order, and Service. By the authority given in this ordination, they are authorized to

---

Continuing in the *BOD*, we find these words: "Beginning in some of the very early Christian communities, the *presbyteros* assisted the bishop in leading the gathered community in the celebration of the sacraments and the guidance and care of its communal life." See *BOD*, ¶ 305, 207. This ministry of assistance has been established subsequent to the ecclesiastical construct known as the "Monarchal Bishop," which itself was subsequent to the first century. It did not exist in the New Testament. Alan Richardson weighs in on this point in his excellent book, *An Introduction to the Theology of the New Testament* when he says, "The priesthood about which the NT speaks is a corporate priesthood of the whole Christian community, and the word (*sacerdis*) priest is never used in respect of any priestly order or caste within the priestly community. All the laity, if we use the word in a biblical way, are priests and ministers of the church of Jesus Christ and all the ministers are equally laymen." Alan Richardson, *An Introduction to the Theology of the New Testament* (New York: Harper & Brothers Publishers, 1958), 301–302.

[202] *BOD*, 209.
[203] *BOD*, 209.
[204] *BOD*, ¶ 333.3, 241.

preach and teach the word of God, to provide pastoral care and counsel, to administer the sacraments of baptism and Holy Communion, and to order the life of the Church for service in mission and ministry."[205] Since 75 percent of United Methodist Churches have 200 members or fewer, this essentially translates into the traditional denominational structure of a single hierarchy required to perform a multiplicity of functions.

In contrast to the amalgamation of centuries of church ecclesiology, the Bible presents a very different picture of local church leadership. To understand the concept of priesthood in the Bible, we must begin in Exodus 19:3-6. Here we find the people of Israel at the foot of Mount Sinai, three months out of bondage to Egypt, and awaiting further instruction. It is here that the Lord God makes an amazing declaration to Moses.

And Moses went up to God, and the Lord called to him out of the mountain, saying,

> Thus you shall say to the house of Jacob, and tell the people of Israel: You have seen what I did to the Egyptians, and how I bore you on eagles' wings and brought you to myself. Now therefore, if you will obey my voice and keep my covenant, you shall be my own possession among all peoples; for all the earth is mine, and you shall be to me a kingdom of priests and a holy nation. These are the words which you shall speak to the children of Israel.

According to this scripture it was the intention of God to make the entire people of Israel the priesthood—to the nations of the world. The two principal functions of the priesthood, of course, were: (1) to represent God to the people (Exod. 34:32-35; Dt. 28:9-10) and (2) to represent the people to God (Exod. 33:12-16; Rom. 9:1-4). In addition, these two primary functions involve amazing intimacy with God; in the Old Testament by Election

---

[205] *BOD*, ¶ 332, 240.

and Covenant, and in the New Testament by the Holy Spirit and Covenant.[206]

The problem with God's original plan as stated was that the people did not cooperate. They did not "obey his voice," and they did not "keep his covenant." Therefore, God went to a kind of plan B, wherein the Lord God appointed the priesthood in Israel from the tribe of Levi and from the family of Aaron.[207] Under this plan, if a Hebrew felt "called to ministry," he would be out of luck if he weren't from the tribe of Levi and the family of Aaron. God makes it very clear to Moses: "They shall join you and attend to the tent of meeting, for all the service of the tent, and no one else shall come near you."[208] Furthermore, "I give you your priesthood as a gift, and anyone else who comes near shall be put to death."[209] And so, the pattern prevailed throughout all the Old Testament period.

There was, however, a preview of coming attractions when we get into the prophetic movement in Israel, particularly with Isaiah. In chapter 61, the prophet foretells big changes on the distant horizon with respect to priesthood. This particular chapter remains one of the high prophetic points in all the Old

---

[206] "The unique element in God's coming in Exodus 19 is not sights and sounds, but the remarkable theological fact that He desires to dwell among His people and to cultivate intimate relations with them. He is the transcendent, supernatural God who, with His power and majesty, is not lightly approached. Yet at the same time, He chose to live among His people and enter into fellowship with them. This is one of the unique features of Israel's God as distinguished from other gods in the ancient near Eastern world. He is transcendent and immanent, supernatural and personal; a God who is high and lifted up, but who also comes to dwell among His people." Allan Coppedge, *The Biblical Principles of Discipleship* (Grand Rapids, MI: Zondervan/Frances Asbury Press, 1989), 37.
[207] See Num. 18:1–7.
[208] Num. 18:4.
[209] Num. 18:7.

104 Biblical Eldership

Testament and is quoted by Jesus in Luke's gospel, chapter 4:18-19. Jesus declared that this very scripture was fulfilled in his own reading of it in the synagogue at Nazareth. Notice verse six, when Isaiah says, "But you shall be called the priests of the Lord; men shall speak of you as the ministers of our God."[210] Following Maundy Thursday, never again was the word "Priest" used to speak of a special caste system within Israel or to what most people would refer to as a clergyman.

As we move into the New Testament, *priest* was used in two distinct ways, first as a term for Jesus, who became the Great High Priest[211] who could offer a once and for all sacrifice for sin: Himself offering the sacrifice and also at the same time being the sacrifice. The second way *priest* is used, following Jesus's death on the cross, is to refer to all those who come to Him to benefit from His grace oblation.[212] These of course are known as

---

[210] This verse refers to Israel as God's son; a collective term used for the people of God.

[211] See Heb. 4:14, 5:5, 7:23, and 7:26. In Heb. 7:16, Jesus's priesthood is clearly established through His passion, death, and resurrection, "an indestructible life." Further, "the Levitical priests under the Mosaic law were determined according to *sarkikes*, a term which relates to the flesh. Here it is used not in reference to the sin nature but in regard to the fact that Aaronic priests were determined by their descent. There is the implication that the priesthood passed from one generation to another. Levitical priests died and were succeeded by their descendants. The 'new Priest,' however, exists not by commandment but by power. And what a power it is: the power not of death and succession, but 'the power of an endless life.' Not just any life, but life which is *akatalutou*, life which cannot be dissolved. He lives forever!" Paul O. Wright, Ph.D., *The Complete Biblical Library: Hebrews* (Springfield, MO: World Library Press, 1990), 83.

[212] See 1 Peter 2:5, 9. Here Peter refers "to the priesthood collectively as a 'royal rank' of priests or the 'body of priests,' i.e., the priestly order. This word *hierateuma* is not found in pre-Christian writings. In the New Testament all believers are called to be priests and minister of the Most High God." *The Complete Biblical Library: Greek-English Dictionary, zeta-kappa* (Springfield, MO: World Library Press, 1990), 145.

Christians (Acts 11:26) and are referred to in 1 Peter 2:5, 9:

> Come to him, to that living stone, rejected by men but in God's sight chosen and precious, and like living stones be yourselves built into a spiritual house, to be a holy priesthood, to offer spiritual sacrifices acceptable to God through Jesus Christ.

Continuing with this understanding, the capstone is put on in Revelation 1:6b and 5:10.[213] The Apostle says, "To him who has loved us, and freed us from our sins by his blood and made us a kingdom of priests to his God and Father, to him be glory and dominion forever and ever." And finally we are reminded that by Jesus's blood and death, a people were ransomed from "every tribe and tongue and people and nation, and has made them a kingdom of priests to our God, and they shall reign on the earth" (Rev. 5:10). This became one of the central issues that launched the Protestant Reformation and Martin Luther to a lifetime of castigation by the Catholic Church.[214]

A final thought on priesthood and its tie to Biblical Eldership is with the understanding of discernment. I have experienced a critical benefit in the functioning of elders in the local church in the area of discernment.

In the Old Testament, a critical function of the priesthood was to discern between the holy and the common. Ezekiel 44:23 says,

---

[213] Realizing that biblical scholarship has assigned the apostle John's writing on the Island of Patmos to dates following A.D. 90, this could well have been the understanding into the second century.

[214] "The distinction between priest and laity plays no part at all, in fact, to put it ever more explicitly: God's grace is shown in the very fact that Jesus calls men to service, particularly whose capacity for it was denied by the Pharisees (Mk. 2:14). This on principle, everyone is engaged in service and there is no point in distinguishing between ordinary believers and those called to service; how could one do so in a band of people whose fundamental service is readiness for suffering and self-sacrifice?" Eduard Schweizer, *Church Order in the New Testament* (Eugene, OR: Wipf & Stock Publishers, 1961), 31–32.

"They shall teach my people the difference between the holy and the common, and show them how to distinguish between the unclean and the clean." I understand this to be a priority of God for His people in covenant relationship throughout history. The Bible substantiates two distinct paths of living before the Lord God, which in turn lead to two very different destinations. [215]

Jay Adams succinctly reminds us of God's purpose to alert the Jew:

> To the fact that all day long, every day, in whatever he does, he must consciously choose God's way. Choices about food, clothing, farming techniques, justice, health care, holidays, and methods of worship were made either God's way or some other way. In other words, the clean/unclean system was designed to develop in God's people an antithetical mentality.[216]

Granted, much of this is linked to ceremonial procedure as it relates to religious law. That is clearly seen in Leviticus 10:10. However, in a world where the boundaries have been erased, how important is the function of discernment among the leadership of the church to have a similar mindset? James reminds us that "religion that is pure and undefiled before God and the Father is this, to visit orphans and widows in their affliction, and to keep oneself unstained from the world." And in chapter four he adds, "Friendship with the world is enmity with God."

Isaiah reminds us that God's ways are not our ways (Isa. 55:8-9), and the Proverbs lift up the wisdom that "the wise of heart is called a man of discernment" (Prov. 16:21). Modern education

---

[215] This is clearly seen in Matthew 7: 13–14: "Enter by the narrow gate; for the gate is wide and the way is easy that leads to destruction, and those who enter by it are many. For the gate is narrow and the way is hard, that leads to life, and those who find it are few."

[216] Jay Adams, *A Call to Discernment: Distinguishing Truth from Error in Today's Church* (Eugene, OR: Harvest House Publishers, 1987), 32.

stresses that truth and values are not absolute but relative. We have been conditioned to "continuum thinking."[217] In modern education this is passed on as values clarification. In the church it is sold as situation ethics. Most have been so saturated by not only the educational ethos, but also newspapers, magazines, radio, television, the Internet; it is no wonder we find ourselves swimming in a sea of relativity.

One could go on and on with biblical teaching at this point; however, I have experience "out in the field" of the benefit of a group of elders who have been schooled in the ways of God. When they find themselves responsible to govern over key aspects of a congregation's journey, discernment is vital for congregation health. Paul says, "And it is my prayer that your love may abound more and more, with knowledge and all discernment" (Phil. 1:9). Even though we have the Holy Spirit and are Christians, discernment is not automatic. God's ways have to be learned. They cannot be discerned if they are not first learned. Hebrews 5:11–14 clearly substantiates this truth.

Unless and until we employ a much broader group of people to these ministry functions in the Body of Christ, we will continue to limp along, wearing out our clergy and limiting our reach for Jesus to a dying world. A return to the biblical understanding of priesthood will move the church light years ahead in ministry effectiveness.[218]

---

[217] "According to continuum thinking, the mode of thinking taught outside the church (and largely within), every idea is a shade of gray. There is no right and wrong or true or false, but only shades of right and wrong or true and false spread along a continuum. The poles of this continuum are extended so far out toward the wings that for all practical purposes they are unattainable and therefore worthless. Nothing then, is wholly right or wrong. All is relative; most of it is subjective." Adams, *Call to Discernment,* 30. One of the most popular books on the market today is titled *Fifty Shades of Grey.* It is all about sexual promiscuity.

[218] Joan Gray, a moderator of the 217th General Assembly of the

Biblical Authority in Leadership versus Traditional Ordination Orders

Given that the ordained ministry is a settled, ecclesiastically approved ministry in virtually all the mainline denominations, the question remains, is it the best approach to full-time service in the local church? For instance, in the UMC, the ordained elder's authority in ministry flows directly from the ordination orders. "The responsibilities of elders are derived from the authority given in ordination."[219] Considering the breadth and depth of such responsibilities (see note 5, introduction), is it really feasible that one ordained elder can proleptically accomplish such variegated tasks?[220] Furthermore, the widely accepted design of putting all the marbles into one basket has

---

Presbyterian Church (USA) and an adjunct faculty member at Columbia Theological Seminary, has it right when she says: "Read the book of Acts and you will enter a world of churches without clergy, at least without clergy as we know that profession. The ancient church was basically lay led." Joan Gray, *Spiritual Leadership for Church Officers: A Handbook* (Louisville, KY: Geneva Press, 2009), ix.

[219] BOD, ¶ 340, 250.

[220] Pastor Daniel Sherman has compiled an impressive list of "burnout causes" for those in the ministry. Having been a full-time pastor for many years, he speaks from direct experience as well as scientific polling. He says that most authors condense causes for pastor burnout into four or five causes. In response to this, Pastor Sherman says, "I'm afraid I can't even get close to that. I started writing and all I could simplify causes of burnout to was 53." See Daniel Sherman, "Pastor Burnout: The Silent Killer," *PastorBurnout.com*, accessed October 10, 2012, http://www.pastorburnout.com/. A smattering of these causes include: administrative burnout, family burnout, expectations burnout, financial pressures burnout, conflict burnout, sin burnout, self-perception burnout, theological burnout, psychological burnout, spiritual burnout, schedule burnout, clergy health issues burnout, and many more. Under each cause Pastor Sherman lists multiple bullet headings.

become highly inefficient in a complicated and technologically governed world, not to mention it is simply outdated.[221] No one person can accomplish so many tasks and remain "intact" at the same time. One may have the authority to execute these responsibilities. Perhaps we have short-circuited the process.[222]

This study argues for a better design, fully biblical in scope and more efficient: Biblical Eldership. The Apostle Paul's appeal in Rom. 12:4-8 and 1 Cor. 12:12-26 is a plea for a multidimensional body ministry, "so that the members may have the same care for one another."[223] By spreading the ministry out among the Body, and allowing others to assume responsibilities

---

[221] Bob Russell, who pastors one of the largest churches in America (Southeast Christian Church in Louisville, KY, with 14,000 attending), weighs in on the overload question in ordained ministry. He says, "The traditional view is that the pastor does the work (of ministry) seen in Eph. 4:11-12," and yet, "One of the keys to advancing the gospel is for the church to be made up of individuals who consider it their task to do the work of ministry rather than having the congregation of people who expect the paid staff to minister to them. No longer is there to be a distinction between clergy and laity, all God's people are to be ministers; we are all priests …" Bob Russell, *When God Builds a Church: 10 Principles for Growing a Dynamic Church* (Louisville, KY: Howard Publishing Co., 2000), 175.

[222] "The Reformation placed great emphasis on the pure preaching of the Word and the right administration of the sacraments as the true marks of the church. To the present, these notes are often stressed as the essence of the Protestant understanding of the church. Yet who but theologically trained clergy were capable of such 'pure' preaching? And who but the ordained clergy could 'rightly' administer the sacraments? If this is what the church is, the laymen can listen to the preaching and receive the sacraments, but their own priesthood is not evident." Georgia Harkness, *The Ministry of the Laity* (Nashville, TN: Abingdon Press, 1962), 71.

[223] 1 Cor. 12:25. The New Living Translation says, "This makes for harmony among the members, so that all the members care for each other." When one considers the current approach of multisite ministry, this becomes even more assiduous to track.

110 Biblical Eldership

that have traditionally been targeted for "ordained clergy," a plethora of needs will be met in the process and the Body will be built up.[224]

In addition, the gifting available to meet all these needs of the Body will be governed by the Holy Spirit and distributed at His will.[225] Biblical Eldership can then be a first positive step at navigating the many demands of local church ministry in the twenty-first century. It is in this modality that the local church can replicate the ministry of Jesus. Experience has verified that a person who is ministering in his or her "function" in the Body of Christ will experience the maximum degree of effectiveness with the minimum degree of frustration. When properly established[226]

---

[224] Juan Carlos Ortiz, a gifted and prolific international evangelist, reminds us in his classic book *A Call to Discipleship*, "Most church congregations are not a spiritual building, but a mountain of bricks. However, good the materials may be, if they are not situated in their right place and correctly related to one another, there is no building" (p. 26). "If Jesus didn't make more than twelve disciples, how can I make several hundred? He himself took just twelve and taught them very well and told these twelve afterwards, 'You go now and make disciples. Do the same thing I did with you.' That is the only way the bricks can become a building, the members a body" (p. 31). And, finally, Ortiz gives this final insight: "In both Catholic and evangelical churches, there is a marked difference between 'clergy' and 'laity.' In this classical relationship, the believers pay a salary to the pastor who in turn offers his services—preaching, visiting, performing ceremonies and organizing committees. But the pastor-layman concept is not biblical. God wants to have a kingdom of priests. We are all priests" (p. 27). Juan Carlos Ortiz, *A Call to Discipleship* (Plainfield, NJ: Logos International, 1975), 26-31.

[225] "Christians live by a messianic epistemology based on immediate revelation by the Holy Spirit as its ideal—even central—characteristic, as Isa. 11:2-3 shows. The mandate, then, is to hear God's immediate voice, which usually commands the hearer to live out an experience of God's might working against opposition and testing. Scripture describes this process as faith." Ruthven, *What's Wrong*, 2-3.

[226] "Thirteen times in the New Testament the word translated 'established' is used, often in the sense of 'set in its proper place'; or as

the body ministry prevails without being culturally conditioned, theologically credentialed, or denominationally configured. These gifts, properly distributed, allowed the church to grow and prosper in her first 350 years, transcending cultural barriers, language barriers, ethnic barriers, geographical barriers, and more.[227]

Supernatural Ministry Construct: Prophetically Driven versus A Cultural Construct: Sociologically Driven

For many in today's church, the unfolding of the Gospel so as to produce fruit in ministry[228] that one can track consistently is

---

'strengthening' or 'shoring up' one's position in the Christian life. In our Romans passage (Rom. 1:7-11) it seems to mean that the *charism* ('grace thing,' spiritual gift) is intended not only to 'strengthen,' but to 'put [the believer] in the proper place' in the charismatic body (Rom. 6; 1 Cor. 12). Note that charismatic empowerment is the object of Paul's prayer for the Roman church, as it is in his other epistles." Ruthven, *What's Wrong*, 164.

[227] Again George Barna gives insight to the importance of lay discipleship: lamenting the high cost of theological education, rising debt among those being trained for ministry, and the recession helping to provide a glut of unemployed clergy, Barna makes this observation: "The upside of these hardships is that churches are relearning how to engage congregants in ministry. Returning to the biblical notion of the priesthood of the laity, more churches are finding that they are capable of maintaining their ministry presence and practices without relying on trained professionals to lead. In the long run, this will serve churches and communities well." George Barna, *Futurecast* (Austin, TX: Barna/Tyndale House Publishers, 2011), 192.

[228] Ruthven, *What's Wrong*, 35. "We all agree that the ultimate goal is intimacy and relationship with God, but what is ignored—even denied—in traditional theology is the process (direct, immediate, prophetic communication with God) of getting there. The message and goal the Bible emphasizes, then, is the process of the Spirit of God revealing God's heart." Intimacy and availability are vital for the prophetic to work.

sociologically construed.[229] Take, for instance, individual church models. A smorgasbord of church models play themselves out across the mainline spectrum and are utilized as overall approaches in ministry. There is the cell-based model, the program-based model, the purpose-driven model, the apostolic model, and the blended model, to name a few. There is nothing inherently wrong with such models because they are designed to connect with the spiritual needs of people at a deeper level. However, by assuming any given model, one more or less closes the door for other options that the Holy Spirit may want to display.[230] If one were to extrapolate out from this one example, one could come up with an endless number of factors to intentionally mold the local church. These factors of rational diagnostics, programs, resources, methodologies, demographics, finances, attendance patterns, gender considerations, and the like are all mixed together in a theological serving bowl to produce what sociologist Georg Ritzer has coined the "McDonaldization" of the church.[231] This McDonaldization process has crept into the

---

[229] Many approaches to ministry in the twenty-first century, by and large, incorporate a cultural analysis involving a rationalistic approach utilizing programs, resources, methodologies, demographics, finances, attendance patterns, and others for the purpose of accentuating ministry effectiveness at the local church address.

[230] Reggie McNeil in his widely read book, *Six Questions for the Church*, weighs in on the sociological mindset relative to church identity: "I believe the search for models can often short-circuit a significant part of a leader's journey into obedience to God. The Bible is not a book of models; it is a record of radical obedience of people who listened and responded to the direction of God for their lives." Reggie McNeil, *The Present Future: Six Tough Questions for the Church* (San Francisco, CA: Jossey-Bass, 2003), xix.

[231] Ritzer is quoted in *The Future of Christianity* as he unpacks his concept. The term "McDonaldization of American culture" is "the process by which the principles of the fast food restaurant are coming to dominate more and more sectors of American society." This process incorporates four defining characteristics: efficiency, calculability,

culture of the Body of Christ in America, and many are pursuing it full-bore. The result is a canned approach to church marketing in order to lure prospective members using family language and symbols. Much of this has already been seen in the church-growth philosophy over the last thirty years.[232] And yet the influence of Christianity in America continues to wane in the process.

A challenge to the cultural approach as seen in the denominational world is the supernatural ministry construct. Philip Jenkins in his epic book, *The Next Christendom*, has firmly established that the center of gravity for Christianity worldwide has shifted from the Western world to Africa, Asia, and the Global South.[233] This "majority world" is already moving in the supernatural, and the church is exploding in these geographical areas of the world.

---

predictability, and control (p. 50). He goes on to say, "These are the moral values of the production line, not of living human beings"—and they have, he argues, "come to shape western society as a whole, with disturbing results" (p. 51). However, this being said—"a product has been identified; [a]nd the quest begins to be able to create, deliver, and market that product as effectively and as efficiently as possible" (p. 50). Alister McGrath, *The Future of Christianity* (Oxford, England: Blackwell Publishers, 2002). This explains, in part, why many churches today offer "delivery systems," which, if packaged correctly, can draw thousands of people to the church building.

[232] "One of the unfortunate side effects of the church growth movement was increased competition between congregations." As a result of this, "an entire industry of church growth experts, seminars, tape clubs, journals, and books all target church leaders who want to up fit their congregations to be competitive in the church market. Churches have jumped headlong into the customer service revolution. Many have purposefully studied the unchurched population to determine the best ways to be 'seeker-sensitive' or 'seeker-driven.' Buildings have been renovated or constructed to satisfy an increasingly high-maintenance church consumer" McNeil, *The Present Future*, 24.

[233] Philip Jenkins, *The Next Christendom: The Coming of Global Christianity* (Oxford, England: Oxford University Press, 2002), 2.

R. L. Lowery, in his stunning book *Walking in the Supernatural,* makes the following claim: "There is no way we will be able to convince the world that Jesus came to earth, destroyed the works of the devil, died on the cross for our sins, rose from the dead, and has the power to save, heal, and deliver today without a manifestation of his miracle-working power in our midst."[234]

I have written elsewhere that "The Bible is a record of the supernatural in our midst. The history of God's people cannot be explained in any other way."[235]

The Word of God is more than a book of doctrine and abstract truth about God. We must engage the text as if God wants to do the same with us as He did with those we read about in the Bible, who were common, ordinary people who God apprehended for His glory and purposes in the earth. We must see their experience as basically the same as ours. If we fail to have this

---

[234] R. L. Lowery, *Walking in the Supernatural* (New Kensington, PA: Whitaker House Publishers, 2007), 265. Lowery goes on to say, "When Jesus returned to the Father, He sent the Holy Spirit to live and remain in them. With the coming of the Holy Spirit, the authority and power to work miracles in His name remained in Jesus's followers. Although Christ no longer was with them in His physical body, they did mighty works through the Holy Spirit and in the authority of Jesus's name." (p. 273)

[235] Scott Kelso, *Let's See What Sticks: Kingdom Living in Chaotic Times* (Enamclaw, WA: WinePress Publishers, 2013), 34. The author continues: "Please refer to this partial list taken from THE BOOK: Dreams, visions, tongues with interpretations, revelations, trances, prophesying, healings, trembling, prostrations, and numerous other wonders—such as iron floating to the surface of a body of water at the command of the prophet; a sun dial standing still; angels breaking open prison doors; earthquakes swallowing people up in judgment; tax money in the mouths of fish; 5000 people fed with just a few morsels of food; people being raised from the dead—even after several days in the grave; walking on water; and on and on."

feeling of identification, the things that happened in the Bible will be distant history and remain unreal to us.[236]

As wonderful as these truths are, perhaps the greatness of God's power is not what He can accomplish through us, but rather what He has done in us. His desire for intimacy through the prophetic is no less astounding and of course qualifies as supernatural. Dr. Jon Ruthven's book, quoted earlier, makes an amazing statement concerning the prophetic: "The testimony of Jesus is the spirit of prophecy (Rev. 19:10) — the scripture describes our thesis, that we are not to substitute any means of communication (angels, saints, doctrines, documents) in place of one's embracing of the 'true words of God,' and that embracing is essentially to worship God."[237]

In many respects, the Hebrew concept of God elicited an awe-filled reverence or respect for the sovereign, almighty God. In the Hebrew tradition, God was the glory behind the veil; however, God was distant in His Almightiness. He was the God who wrapped the mountain in smoke and fire, while demanding that Moses take off his shoes in his presence. Yet when Jesus approached this God, He called Him Father, ABBA, and Daddy. For Jesus, speaking directly to His Father was a safe place of intimacy, modeled for His disciples and for us (Matt. 6:9–13).

Today we think it natural to approach God as Father; however, 2,000 years ago in Palestine, this kind of intimate language was controversial. In John 8, the Pharisees were ready to stone Jesus to death for referring to His Father as ABBA (John 8:59). Yet, this intimacy is one of the major works that God wants to accomplish in our lives. And from it flows the mighty works of God.

---

[236] Kelso, *Let's See*, 101–102.
[237] Ruthven, *What's Wrong*, 291.

Conclusion

As we move into the future, the church has some spiritual due diligence to accomplish. I am not referring to bigger buildings, more professional staff, denominational mergers, better programs and methods, and multisite locations. I refer rather to a time-honored tryst with the Almighty, namely soul-searching. Instead of scurrying around and doing busy-work ministry, we need to seek again the prophetic flow from a supernatural God and hear again His lovely voice, distinctive from all others. In this, God has reminded us from 2 Chronicles 16:9, "For the eyes of the Lord run to and fro throughout the whole earth, to show his might in behalf of those whose heart is blameless toward him."

4

Methodology

Introduction

A STUDY IN BIBLICAL ELDERSHIP is in part a study in structure. *Webster's* defines structure as "the arrangement or interrelation of all the parts of a whole *(n)*; to put together systematically; to construct *(v)*."[238] Most things that are functional contain structure. An automobile has a frame; a house has a foundation; an athletic competition has a playing field. Even the church is "built upon the foundation of the apostles and prophets, Christ Jesus himself being the chief cornerstone" (Eph. 2:20).

In addition, if there is one thing Christian denominations are known for, it is structure; however, it has been mitigated from the first-century pattern and changed just enough to accommodate a syncretism removed from the days of the apostles. For example, "the Episcopal church emphasizes the role of a bishop or overseer (that is, the Archbishop of Canterbury) as a ruler, whereas the Presbyterians favor the role of elder (with classes of presbyters or elders)."[239]

---

[238] *Webster's New Universal Unabridged Dictionary*, 2nd ed., s.v. "structure."
[239] Neil Cole, *Primal Fire: Reigniting the Church with the Five Gifts of Jesus*

The problem in initiating Biblical Eldership in the local church could be formidable. Most churches already have an established protocol for ecclesiological administration. "Kicking against the goads" of traditional church leadership could result in a nugatory challenge. The doctrine of the priesthood of the believer has been received in principle throughout the UMC, the implementation of it based on Ephesians 4:12-13. However, because of our legacy from the Protestant Reformation, the pastoral leadership is solitary in most cases and open to numerous pitfalls. When we turn to scripture, the Lord God knew early on that Moses needed a plurality of leadership to administer to the people. Hence, a prophetic design of elders was initiated among God's people.

The data from this project suggests that pastors, who employ an eldership design as evidenced herein, will receive some needed relief from their anxious feeling of being depleted and frustrated in ministry. When Biblical Eldership is employed, a trained group of leaders comes alongside the pastor to lift up his/her arms (Exod. 17:12) in the heat of battle. These elders, as proposed, have helped the pastor shoulder the ministry in the local context. One could imagine the present design extrapolated in multiple settings with positive results. As a consequence, this project carries the possibility to enliven local church leadership, promote vital Christianity, and enhance the spiritual government of Christ's church on earth.

In the first chapter of this dissertation, we have defined our ministry focus, established the theoretical foundation for the ministry project, and examined the relevant literature on the subject. In this chapter we will begin by stating the hypothesis, followed by a discussion of the research design. The research

---

(Carol Stream, IL: Tyndale Momentum, 2014), 284.

design will yield the data to be measured, and finally we will verify the instrumentation used to extract the data." Validity will emerge from the final narrative description present in the ministry setting."[240]

Hypothesis

The problem is that Christian ministry carries with it one of the highest causality rates of any profession in society. Scores of pastors leave ministry every month due to overwork, underpay, and being inadequately equipped to negotiate the contemporary world of eroding moral boundaries. We are in need of a new paradigm[241] of ministry based on new hermeneutics of biblical understanding concerning the gifts of the Holy Spirit and the unfolding of God's action in history through the prophetic outpouring mentioned by the prophet Isaiah (59:20-21), and confirmed at Pentecost (Acts 2:1-39).

Therefore, this project has tested a template to call and disciple a group of leaders in the local church who function as elders after the pattern given in Numbers 11 and 1 Peter 5:1-5. These elders come alongside the pastor for the purpose of spiritual oversight and congregational ministry. This project tested the hypothesis that pastors and elders, who have engaged in nine months of training for biblical leadership, will develop and be released in the following ministry behaviors: Christian

---

[240] William R. Myers, *Research in Ministry: A Primer for the Doctor of Ministry Program,* rev. ed. (Chicago, IL: Sage Publications, 2000), 29.

[241] For the next many years, the church will continue to be in a mode of reinventing itself while it escapes a fifteenth-century Protestant Reformation paradigm and moves forward toward a twenty-first century presentation. The present research intends to weigh in on this discovery process. What the end result will eventually look like is still to be determined.

conversion, physical healing, deliverance, and prayer counseling with individuals in their church and community. The project utilized a grounded theory framework, as well as employed a phenomenological structure of inquiry. The methods for data collection were pre- and post-test questionnaires, personal journals, and pastoral exit interviews.

Research Design

The research method chosen for this project is an action research collaborative design. It has been anticipated that the participants will be involved in generating the information[242] as they experience "eldership" for the first time in their lives. Working with a group of five pastors (churches), the writer did "presuppose" that each person's ideas are equally significant as potential resources for creating interpretive categories of analysis.[243] This design has attempted to analyze the social reality (the big picture) of Biblical Eldership in the local church.

I used a qualitative research approach using a grounded theory framework at points employing a phenomenological structure of inquiry. The qualitative approach will allow for "the data to be collected in the participants' own setting; using data analysis inductively building from particular to general themes, and the researcher making interpretation of the meaning of the data."[244] Therefore, the researcher "seeks to establish the meaning of phenomenon from the views of the participants."[245] A phenomenological structure of inquiry will allow the researcher

---

[242] John W. Creswell, *Research Design: Qualitative, Quantitative and Mixed Methods Approaches* (Thousand Oaks, CA: SAGE Publications, 2014), 8.
[243] Jackie Bastion, class notes from August 20, 2012.
[244] Creswell, *Research Design*, 4.
[245] Creswell, *Research Design*, 19.

Methodology 121

to probe "experience and phenomenon,"[246] which draw conclusions from participants who have all experienced the same discipleship design—Biblical Eldership for the first time in their churches' history.

In an attempt to ensure the validity of research results, I have triangulated methods of inquiry. Pre- and post- questionnaires have been given to each of the five pastors under study. These questionnaires have measured general categories of ministry and, compared over time, one may see if personal expectations have developed favorably or unfavorably in the context of ministry. This measurement has yielded a "quick quantitative assessment"[247] of ministry expectations and results.

In addition, journals were kept by each of the five pastors over a six-month period. The journals were collected at the end of the six months for coding and analysis and will be kept on site as a permanent part of the project. In addition, "selective interviews"[248] will be recorded from one elder from each of the five churches (each elder chosen by the pastor) and analyzed for data extraction as we test for the four primary areas of ministry: salvation, healing, deliverance, and prayer counseling. Auxiliary data up to four additional categories, such as encouragement to the pastor or growth in intimacy with God among the elders, may yield results not anticipated. These categories may or may not lend themselves to validate the hypothesis. I used five of the eight corporate primary strategies for additional validity to the project. They are triangulation of data; member checking; rich,

---

[246] Creswell, *Research Design*, 14.
[247] Meyers, *Research in Ministry*, 62.
[248] Creswell, *Research Design,* 190. As Creswell states and the researcher has done, "These interviews involve unstructured and generally open-ended questions that are few in number and intended to elicit views and opinions from the participants."

thick description; bias of the researcher; and negative or discrepant information.[249]

The Role of the Researcher

Because I chose a proactive research design, I interfaced with the participants at several points in the process. Context associates were used to interface with the participants at strategic points in the process. Directing this process involved teaching, advising, clarifying, and encouraging the participants to faithful discipleship. Biblical Eldership involves accountability not only to God but to the congregation in which they serve. Points of tension may be inevitable because the insertion of elders into congregational ministry will inevitably change the ministry dynamic in the congregation. The lead pastor of each church has functioned as the go-between in this unfolding ministry experiment.

Admittedly, the entire project has come out of the researcher's own experience in ministry, and positive replication and results are anticipated for the end of the process. Given these parameters, a bias is built into the process by the researcher. As William Creswell intimates, personal value assumptions and bias are well intact as the researcher approaches the chosen project.[250] Many of these values have been forged out of the fire of real ministry with real people over a thirty-year period of time. One cannot claim total objectivity in the project. The ministry of Biblical Eldership has great potential to transform the face of ministry across the participant congregations as this form of discipleship unfolds. I anticipate that the social reality (the big picture) of Biblical Eldership will benefit both the pastors and the

---

[249] Creswell, *Research Design*, 201-202.
[250] Creswell, *Research Design*, 202. Creswell says, "Good qualitative research contains comments by the researchers about how their interpretation of the findings is shaped by their background, such as gender, culture, history, and socioeconomic origin."

churches under study, in ways yet to be determined. I believe this project holds out hope for an entire denomination (United Methodist) often imprisoned by low self-esteem, theological conflict, and discouragement in professional ministry.

Having said this, the present project is designed to allow the data to speak accurately and objectively as the project unfolded over a six-month period of time. Through consistent modes of measurement, careful field notes, and personal testimonies of ministry development, the writer has established the theory of Biblical Eldership as "grounded." The correlation of total data derived from five individual congregations has yielded to measureable, reliable results.

Measurement

As stated previously, the bulk of this project has been conducted on site at five different church locations. Four of the churches are denominational and one is nondenominational. They span the spectrum from large churches of over 1,000 in attendance to medium-size churches of 300 in attendance, to smaller churches of less than 200 in attendance. The demographics of the churches range from urban to suburban to county seat in location.[251] Each church has extended the study of Biblical Eldership voluntarily with a good deal of anticipation.

This study includes three primary components of data collection to comply with triangulation parameters, namely, a pre-test corresponding to a similar post-test given to the senior pastors; a journal distributed to each pastor, which was used over a six-month period; and finally an on-site visit with each elders group with field notes, including an interview with one of the elders chosen by the senior pastor. Corollary arrangements included a site visit to Trinity Family Life Center during an in-

---

[251] Please see Appendix A.

session ministry experience with their elder team, allowing for interaction and de-briefing. I have taken field notes in said sessions. In addition, a group of four Trinity Elders (context associates) have been available to travel to participant sites for counsel and further training in Biblical Eldership.

The pre-test is composed of open-ended questions with the hope of yielding the greatest amount of information possible. The pre-test was administered on site at Trinity Family Life Center on March 27, 2014, to all five pastors at the same time. A similar post-test was administered during the month of July 2014 (see Appendix C).

I distributed journals to each pastor at the time of the pre-test questionnaire, so that each senior leader could record relevant impressions, thoughts, and experiences, including the value of the "big picture" of Elders Ministry and its benefit to their local church. In addition, each pastor led his or her group of elders in a study of the book *Biblical Eldership* by Alexander Strauch[252] early in the process, in order to give grounding to the experience and a heads-up for their ministry protocol.

The research protocol called for at least one on-site session with the Elders of Trinity Family Life Center in context—observing an actual session of prayer for salvation, healing, or deliverance, or prayer counseling with a prescheduled recipient. Sessions were followed by a debriefing time that included questions and answers. All five churches traveled at their own expense to the site for the sessions.

Finally, I interviewed each church's senior pastor and head elder in their locations. These sessions were voice recorded and transcribed verbatim for analysis and coding. It should be noted that this entire process has made every effort to ensure the privacy of the participants[253] (see Appendix D).

---

[252] Strauch, *Biblical Eldership*.
[253] Creswell, *Research Design*, 99.

Data Analysis and Interpretation

I believe that the range of data-collection strategies mentioned above did yield a solid general understanding of the experience of Biblical Eldership in a congregation for the first time. Examination was given to similar and dissimilar patterns that arose through the process. Open and selective coding in triangulation did allow for emergent themes and patterns to be identified. I examined similar patterns across the five churches. In this way the data may suggest what may work for a larger group such as an entire denomination. Perhaps one will be able to build a mosaic of this form of discipleship for the local church in general. As negative patterns were discovered, they added validity to the project.

I am most interested in understanding the effect of Biblical Eldership in the local setting on a measurable increase as self-reported salvation, healing, deliverance, and prayer counseling, while at the same time increasing intimacy with God. Auxiliary component variables such as encouragement to the pastor, personal accountability among the elders, congregational stability, and growth in intimacy with God among the elders themselves were recorded and evaluated. Through this process, a "grounded theory" has emerged concerning Biblical Eldership in the local church and its consequences for charismatic ministry.

Finally, I have shared the results of the research with the five churches in an attempt to see if they indeed paralleled the experience of the participants. The findings have been corroborated with the context associates in order to confirm (or not confirm) the emergent patterns of the project. We will want to answer the question: "Does the final understanding concerning Biblical Eldership comport with the experience in the field of the peer associates, the participants, and the researcher, verifying 'grounded theory'?"

5

Field Experience

Introduction

THIS EXPERIMENT TESTED the hypothesis that "pastors and elders who have engaged in a six-month training for Biblical Eldership will develop and be released in the following ministry behaviors: Christian conversion, physical healing, deliverance, and prayer counseling with individuals in their church and community. In addition, four auxiliary areas of development were of primary interest: anointing in ministry, humility, confidence in ministry, and expectation in ministry.

This chapter represents the results of the above project in three basic stages. The first section will explain the analytical process involved in the template along with methodology. The second section will look at the demographics of the pastors involved in the study. The third section will present the actual findings (analysis) of the data with implications and conclusion.

The Template Design

The project commenced on March 27, 2014 at 1:00 P.M. in the building of Trinity Family Life Center (UMC) in Pickerington, Ohio. Five pastors within a 150-mile radius of the United Theological Seminary in Dayton, Ohio, agreed to raise up Biblical Eldership in their churches. At this time, I administered a pre-test questionnaire relative to each pastor's leadership style and the history of ministry in their present church. The questionnaire was designed to extract relevant initial information concerning the pastor's context in ministry. Toward the end of the project, the pre-test questionnaire was merged with a similar post-test questionnaire to compare and examine data relative to their results in the field. Five additional questions were added to the post-test to secure the data. The post-test was e-mailed to all five participants early in July 2014 and appointments with me were scheduled for the week of July 21, 2014.

In addition, I passed out spiral notebook journals so the participants could keep a log of their reflections, insights, testimonies, and feedback from both their congregations and the elders who emerged in the process. They were encouraged to use the journals as diaries for recording new experiences and insights as the project progressed.

A third component to retrieve information was an actual face-to-face exit interview with each pastor and one of their elders of choice. During this concluding exit interview, I told each pastor that I would be available to work with their new "elder template" as far into the future as they needed. The interviews were voice recorded and transcribed following the session. Five specific questions were asked of each pastor having successfully gone through the project. The questions were: (1) What was it like for you to go through this process of raising up Biblical Eldership in your church? (2) Would you do it again in a different context? (3) Would you recommend this experience to other pastors? (4) Was there any downside to the process for you or your people? (5) Where do you see yourself going from here? Herein, each voice recording was transcribed for analysis. Each interview response was spontaneous with no preempting.

The first meeting with anyone associated with this project was on November 4, 2013. At that time, I had twelve possible prospects to go through the study. The following five months would produce five solid candidates. However, at the November meeting, which was a recruiting event, a protocol was given in writing to all prospective pastors so that they could get a head start on recruitment if they knew they would be participating. Again, the motivation for the protocol was taken from God's instruction to Moses in Numbers 11:16–17 and was actually conceived during the researcher's experience as a pastor in the field.

The basic protocol is as follows. I first encouraged the pastors to preach on Numbers 11, with emphasis on elder ministry. At the conclusion of the service, index cards were distributed to each person in attendance. The congregation was encouraged to write one name on the card as a suggestion of a person whom they felt would be qualified to serve as an elder with the pastor in ministry. Remember, God told Moses to choose seventy elders "who you know to be elders among the people." In other words, these people would have existent qualifications even though they didn't have the title. Over the following few weeks, the pastor would pray over the cards and invite the first elder. As the process continued, these two then would pray and perhaps fast and appoint two more from the names given by the congregation. The same pattern is repeated, appointing two elders at a time until the process yielded the desired number for their context in ministry.

Following the completion, the pastor was asked to lead the

new elders through a study of the book *Biblical Eldership* by Alexander Strauch. With this grounding, the new group would be on a firm foundation. Subsequently, the ensuing months (April–July), each elder team was invited to a Monday night meeting of the elders at the home church—Trinity Family Life Center (TFLC) in Pickerington, Ohio. During this two-hour meeting, the project pastors and their new elders could interface with the elders at Trinity (four of whom are the researcher's context associates) and observe them in an actual ministry appointment. During this forty-five-minute appointment, the elders of TFLC would spend time with a pre-designated person who was experiencing some life crisis or who needed counseling or who was facing a difficult decision. This provided the project pastors with real-life experience in context, as well as supplying an important visual for their upcoming ministry in their local church. In addition, they also participated in a question-and-answer debriefing segment following the appointment segment.

Finally, before leaving to go home, the TFLC elders would "commission" the project pastor and his elders with an anointing with oil and prayer. Results of their encounter are given attention late in this chapter through field notes from the researcher.

Demographic Analysis

I assigned fictitious names to the participant pastors to ensure anonymity. In this, five colors designate the pastors: green, blue, brown, gray, and black. These could also be real names of real people so their names are capitalized throughout the report (see Appendix A).

Pastor Green directs a large county seat United Methodist congregation founded in 1857, presently with a membership of 544 members and an average attendance of over 1,000. The worship is contemporary. The church draws from twenty-nine postal zones. Pastor Green is forty-eight years old and has earned the Doctor of Ministry degree. He describes himself as "very conservative" theologically and the congregation the same. The church budget is $1,185,000 and is staff-guided with sixteen full-time and ten part-time employees. The church is a melting pot of different denominational backgrounds with a distinctive group of low-income families. The church has four worship services, encompassing one on Saturday evening. The church is a cell-based congregation with twenty-six active cell groups. The church is covered by several intercessory prayer groups. The building is also used by other community groups. Discipleship patterns are primarily female-based.

Pastor Blue directs a county seat United Methodist congregation of 400 members with 200 in attendance at two Sunday-morning services. The worship is contemporary. The congregation was formed in 1853 and presently draws from forty different postal zones. Pastor Blue is forty-seven years old. The church budget is $560,000 with a staff of three people. The theological index of the pastor is Charismatic/Pentecostal. The theological index of the congregation is Evangelical. The church has been in some decline in the last ten years; however, they recently moved into a new church built on twenty acres of ground. This is not a cell-based church. Discipleship patterns are primarily female-based.

Pastor Brown directs a mission church plant founded in August 1999 in Columbus, Ohio. The congregation is primarily African American immigrants from West Africa with a smattering of white folks. The congregation is 200 members with 150 in attendance in one morning service. They enjoy contemporary worship. The church draws from forty-six postal zones. Pastor Brown is fifty years old with a bachelor's degree and twenty years of experience. The church budget is $200,000, and the church is staff-guided with five on staff. It is a cell-based church. The church is covered by regular intercessory prayer groups. They are presently focusing on leadership training and starting a day-care center. Long-range plans are to build a new sanctuary. The church is also very intentional about reaching the city and continually interfacing with the larger body of Christ in Columbus.

Pastor Gray directs a rural congregation (Assembly of God) of 350 members that was founded on March 24, 2013. The average attendance is 240 in two morning worship services with contemporary worship while excelling in media ministry. The church draws from twenty postal zones and rents a school for their facility. Pastor Gray is thirty-seven years old. The pastor has fifteen years of experience and describes himself as "full gospel/charismatic" theologically and the church as "missional" and committed to the Word of God. The church budget is $150,000 and is staff-guided with three staff members. The congregation is not cell-based but describes itself as "hybrid." The church is regularly covered in intercessory prayer. The church is aggressive evangelically and focused on community outreach with a well-developed online presence. Even though the church has been up and running for only sixteen months, they have won over 200 people to the Lord while adding an average of 100 to the morning services.

Pastor Black directs a United Methodist congregation of 400 members with 245 in attendance at two morning-worship services, one contemporary and one traditional. The church was founded in 1818 and presently draws from three postal zones. The pastor is sixty-six years old and ready for retirement. He has earned the Doctor of Ministry degree. The church is small-town rural. The pastor describes himself as Third Wave theologically and the congregation as mainline evangelical/charismatic. The church budget is $390,000 with a "program-led" volunteer staff. The church is not cell-based but is strong in discipleship and missions. The church is covered regularly by intercessory prayer and strong female leadership and an active men's group.

The Role of the Researcher

Admittedly, the entire project has come out of the researcher's own experience in ministry. Positive replication and results are anticipated for the end of the project. Given these parameters, a bias is built into the process by the researcher. As William Creswell states, "Personal value assumptions and bias are well intact as the research approaches the chosen project." Many of these values have been forged out of real ministry with real people over a thirty-year period of time. Given this history, total objectivity is out of the question. As Miles, Huberman, and Saldana have noted in their comprehensive book on qualitative data analysis, "The words we choose to document what we see and hear in the field can never truly be 'objective'; they can only be our interpretation of what we experience."[254]

Furthermore, I have experienced a long and consistent relationship with other pastors through city-reaching ministries, pastors' retreats, and Bible conferences. Such events have become a staple on the researcher's calendar, attempting, of course, to respond to the call of God. I further believe the office of pastor/teacher represents the key position in the effective functioning of the local church. If the pastor is discouraged and defeated in ministry, the congregation's cup will only be half full. However, if the pastor is encouraged in his or her call, the

---

[254] Matthew B. Miles, A. Michael Huberman, and Johnny Saldana, *Qualitative Data Analysis: A Methods Sourcebook* (Los Angeles, CA: Sage Publications, 2014), 11.

134 Biblical Eldership

congregation may tend to be healthy and vital in its expression of ministry.

Into this mix, a group of elders who are mature, motivated, and excited about Christ's ministry can readily launch and multiply ministry effectiveness alongside the pastor. This we see in the ministry of Jesus (Lk. 10:1-2, 17-20) and the apostles (Acts 15). One would hope that a similar experience would emerge at the conclusion of this project. Locked up in the scripture and the Spirit of God are all the tools one needs for effective ministry.

The ministry of Biblical Eldership has great potential to transform the face of ministry across participant congregations as this form of discipleship unfolds. I anticipate the social reality (the big picture) of Biblical Eldership will benefit both the pastors and the churches under study. Furthermore, I believe the project holds out hope for an entire denomination (United Methodist) often imprisoned by low self-esteem, theological conflict, and discouragement in professional ministry.

Having said this, I am determined to allow the data to speak for itself, with accuracy and objectivity as the following measurement may allow. Through consistent modes of data retrieval, i.e., careful field notes, personal testimonies of ministry development, and creative discipleship, the writer expects the theory of Biblical Eldership to become "grounded."

Data Collection Strategies

The research method chosen for this project is an action research collaborative design. The design is meant to yield strategies of inquiry in a qualitative research approach. "Qualitative data with their emphasis on people's lived experiences are fundamentally well suited for locating the meanings people place on the events, processes, and structures of their lives and for connecting these meanings to the social world around them."[255] The strategies are: pre- and post-questionnaires given to the five participant pastors; personal journals to record strategic events, methods implementation, personal insights, and spiritual growth taking place on a linear timeline; and final exit interviews with the participant pastors and one elder chosen by the pastor. The interviews were voice recorded and transcribed for data retrieval.

I believe that these collection strategies will engage each participant pastor with a clear opportunity to share his experience, insights, challenges, and impressions, generating meaningful data which will be interpreted in a narrative flow. For example, by using the pre-test/post-test vehicle, the participants are free to express their true "before and after" experience in the project. The pre-test was given on March 27, 2014, and the post-test was given on July 7, 2014. The researcher's intention was to compare the pre- and post-test to see if there were changes that had occurred with the insertion of Elder Ministry under the template that was given in the beginning of the project. Positive changes would reveal a successful project; negative changes would yield reason for concern.

Secondly, the use of participant journals yielded real-time event data unique to each pastor and church in the project. This will include "naturally occurring, ordinary events in natural settings, so that we have a strong handle on what 'real life' is like."[256] I explained to the participants that the use of journals was a common and effective tool for data collection in a qualitative study, and each was encouraged to record thoughts, testimonies, and impressions unique to his particular context in ministry. The journals were also distributed on March 27 and

---

[255] Miles et al., *Qualitative Data*, 11.
[256] Miles et al., *Qualitative Data*, 11.

were collected the fourth week of July 2014 during pre-scheduled exit interviews with the researcher.

Finally, I wanted an exit interview with simple open-ended questions that allowed each pastor great flexibility in responding. The voice-recorded conversations yielded solid information in a kind of summary context. (The questions are recorded on page 128.) Through these data collection methods, I believe I received a wonderful "picture" in context of Biblical Eldership and its impact on the pastor, the congregation, and the elders themselves, as well as the community at large. We now turn to the analysis of the data.

Data Analysis

Once the data was collected, I began to break it down church by church, reviewing each church's experience in raising up Biblical Eldership while looking for themes, similar experiences, impressions, and inner-church dynamics at play. Following a few excursions through the data, I began to draw back with a kind of "wide-angle lens," observing the data as a whole. Emergent themes began to repeat themselves throughout the material. Diagnostic codes were assigned to emergent themes. The codes became tags for assigning units of meaning used to decipher the social reality (big picture) of Biblical Eldership. The codes were very useful in organizing the data into segmentation and for further analysis.

In the original abstract, I tested for four primary ministry experiences in Biblical Eldership: salvation, healing, deliverance, and prayer counseling. In addition, the project left room for auxiliary areas of development: anointing in ministry, humility, confidence in ministry, and expectation in ministry. It became apparent early on that the auxiliary areas of ministry development became the primary expression of all the participant pastors and elders as their experience played out, and the four primary ministry experiences noted in the abstract became the auxiliary segments of the data. The reason for this phenomenological development will be forthcoming in the concluding remarks. However, the data is clear on this reversal.

The Codes

The data indicates four major themes embedded in this project on Biblical Eldership. They are: an increase in confidence in ministry (CM); an increase in expectation in ministry (EXP); increase in anointing in ministry (ANT); and the manifestation of humility in eldership (HUM). A brief explanation is in order.

Confidence in ministry is expressed when the new elder embarks on ministry in the authority given to him/her by the pastor of the church. The corporate contribution in supplying the names for elders played out in the template also added to the elders' confidence. Our experience is that when the pastor releases others to minister in his/her "function" in the Body of Christ, that is exactly what happens.

Secondly, expectation in ministry arises from the data. Healthy churches are based on giftings and callings expressed in a balanced body ministry (Eph. 4:1–12; 1 Cor. 12:4–11). Our experience demonstrates that as elders meet weekly and pray confidently for others, fruit is born and expectation increases.

Thirdly, anointing in ministry includes the ability to hear God correctly. This may come primarily through the study of the Word of God and prayer, reflected in a protocol to follow the leading of the Holy Spirit. As a result, others benefit from the ministry of elders (Acts 6:2–4).

Fourthly, our experience demonstrates that humility involves the awareness that one needs to "walk the talk" of the Christian life before one can model or teach it to others. Further, humility is an awareness of God's grace for every ministry encounter whereby Jesus may increase and the elder may decrease (Matt. 10:24–25; 1 Peter 5:5).

In addition, the subthemes embedded in this project include praying in the supernatural, in order that the Holy Spirit will direct the elder toward the ministry needs of others in an atmosphere of love and acceptance. The elder believes and expects God to manifest Himself supernaturally in the ministry context. Furthermore, the data indicates that through a disciplined regimen of training, practicing, and releasing the Holy Spirit to mentor the groups from "one degree of glory to another," the individual elder does experience spiritual growth personally.

Finally, the project asserts a congregational learning curve for Biblical Eldership. This is primarily because the elder template will have been a new experience in virtually every church in the project. Prior to this experiment, eldership was nowhere on their radar. The presence and ministry of elders will alter congregational identity and stability either in a positive direction or a negative direction.

I admit that the major themes and subthemes are at points interconnected and overlapping throughout. However, an attempt has been made to clarify the data through a narrative analysis and coding regimen. The following "findings section" produced each data source: pre- and post-test, participant journals, and final exit interviews with an overlay of the four major themes. The subthemes emerged intermittingly through the composite design of Biblical Eldership in each of the five churches. This way triangulation of data is applied to each of the five churches. Direct quotes, comments, and observations from the participants have appeared throughout the narrative explanation. All grammar and punctuation of original quotes remain intact.

Findings

Confidence in Ministry (CM): Pre-test/Post-test

Questions 2–5, 7, 14, and 20 are directly related to the CM factor in this study (see Appendices B and C). Questions 2–5 were designed to probe the respondent's pre- and post-elder history relative to the four ministry behaviors designated for measurement in the researcher's abstract: salvation, healing, deliverance, and prayer counseling, while questions 7, 14, and 20 measure confidence in overall ministry in general.

Specifically, on questions 2 and 3, all five pastors were deeply confident in the ministry behaviors of salvation and healing. See Figure 5.1:

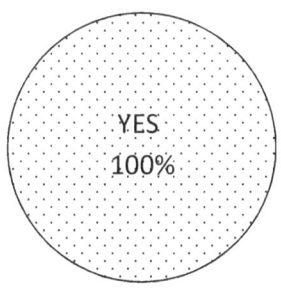

Figure 5.1: Confident behaviors of salvation and healing

Five Pastors

In questions 4 and 5, four out of five pastors were confident in deliverance and prayer counseling. See Figure 5.2:

Figure 5.2: Confident in deliverance
and prayer counseling

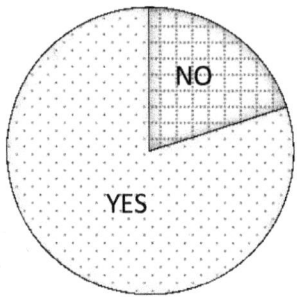

Five Pastors

Question 7 searched the big picture concerning the miraculous in general. Again, four out of five were very confident. See Figure 5.3:

Figure 5.3: Confident in miracles

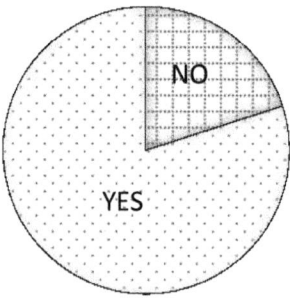

Five Pastors

Pastor Black indicated other up-and-running pre-trained groups for all four ministry behaviors and was not sure if the elders would want to duplicate ministry efforts with those already engaged. With several well-developed ministries already in place and a pastor with nineteen years' experience, the need was obviously being met.

Question 14 was designed to probe "concerns" related to Biblical Eldership. Three out of five pastors were very confident. See Figure 5:4:

Figure 5:4: Confident in Biblical leadership

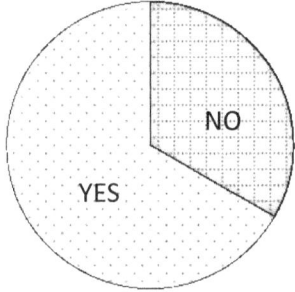

Five Pastors

Pastor Brown and Pastor Blue held concerns around the issue of congregational acceptance of the ministry in general. This is to say, since there was a completely new paradigm for Biblical Discipleship, the congregation would need a longer break-in period in order to understand and accept the ministry. Question 20 is significant because of the one "take away" for each pastor in the project. All five pastors were very upbeat and confident as to elders making a real difference in their outlook and ministry. See Figure 5.5:

Figure 5.5: Confident in elders in
making a real difference

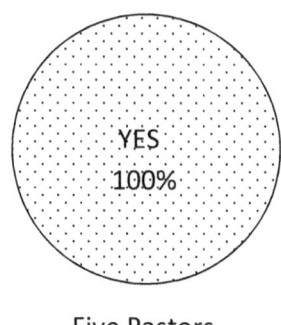

Five Pastors

Direct quotes are as follows:

Pastor Green comments: "Meeting with such a mature group of men, I look forward to our meeting every week. I leave every meeting with a great sense of joy."

Pastor Gray records: "This is a must in the church. My longevity will be protected by using this team for help and ministry."

Pastor Blue says: "The elders meet a tremendous need in the local church for a visible, tangible representation of spiritual vitality and integrity."

Finally, Pastor Black says: "I can already sense in the last few months that we have been together, that this is going to be a major strengthening of my ministry." This one post-test question alone betrays a tremendous blessing experience by each pastor through Biblical Eldership.

Confidence in Ministry (CM): Journals

The journals aptly describe more of the unfolding and interplay of the process in acquiring eldership in each local church. The operative words observed in this unfolding process is confidence and growth in maturity in each setting. I am surprised at how quickly most of all of the groups take hold and apply themselves diligently to their new role. This unfolding process is quite positive and deliberate.

For example, early on Pastor Green had significant pushback from five or six women in the church because there were no female elders on the new elder board. Some of the women were even staff members, which could have caused a prolonged conflict in ministry dynamics. However, one of the women who had expressed reservations concerning the lack of female representation on the elders' board accompanied her friend to visit the elders for prayer. Her friend's back pain had persisted for three weeks; the elders anointed with oil and prayed for healing. Something must have convinced this friend that the elders were for real, because the pastor reports a few days following the above encounter: "She has completely changed her thinking concerning the elders and is now encouraging people to come for prayer" (July 6, 2014).

Pastor Black reports on his first official meeting with his four elders on May 21, 2014: "Met last night with four men starting elder board. There was an automatic connection. We will move forward quickly. They also felt a strong call to be in support of me." Just a week later, Pastor Black records: "Great time of prayer last night. We know each other, but getting to know at a deeper level. This group of four is eager and committed." One month later he continues: "I am realizing very quickly how much I needed this group. There is great support" (June 27, 2014).

Pastor Brown, using his elders in morning worship, records: "Ministered to the needy during the altar call today. And miracles did happen. One woman was healed of chronic back pain instantly" (July 27, 2014).

Confidence in Ministry (CM): Exit Interviews

When asked if the participant pastors would recommend this elder ministry to others, Pastor Green responded: "Yes based on the outcome of the men here, yes absolutely" (July 24, 2014). Pastor Blue responded: "Yeah, absolutely, especially in church structures that do not provide for this" (UMC, et al; July 22, 2014). Pastor Brown said: "I would recommend it to any church. We have some churches that we have planted in the city, and I am looking at the model, so it can work for us" (July 28, 2014). Continuing, Pastor Gray recorded: "I would highly recommend it because…what I love about it is the church gets a diversity of ministry and it's not something encompassed in one man…." (July 23, 2014). Finally, Pastor Black said: "Yes I would!" (July 21, 2012). These comments strike at confidence head on. It appears the ministry has made a profound difference in a relatively short period of time.

Expectation in Ministry (EXP): Pre-test/Post-test

Questions 11–13 probe expectation as one journeys into the future of elder ministry. Question 11 looks at benefits of the ministry in the future. In this category all five pastors expect a shared responsibility in ministry load as they go into the future. This carries with it a "great relief" mentally and physically to the pastor. In addition, three of the five specifically stated a greater stability for the congregation, realizing a kind of gatekeeping function associated with the elders. See Figure 5.6:

Figure 5.6: Expect a shared
responsibility in ministry load

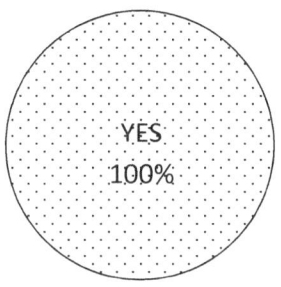

Five pastors

Question 12 touches on any challenges in developing this ministry. Four of the five pastors understand their regular meeting with these men would show progress in their spiritual acumen. See Figure 5.7:

Figure 5.7: Confident that regular meetings
with elders would make a difference

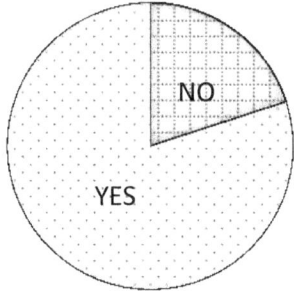

Five Pastors

Pastor Black called it "a work in progress." Pastor Green acknowledged "growth areas as ministry scenarios expand."

Overall, the challenges awaiting the future seem to be positive in scope. Question 13 looks at the "growing edge" in this ministry. Three of the five mentioned ongoing training as an important component for this question. See Figure 5.8:

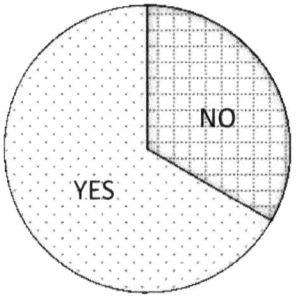

Figure 5.8: Confident that ongoing training would make a difference

Five Pastors

Pastor Brown said "pretty much everything since this is a completely new experience for the church." The data here indicates a growing expectation of the ministry of elders into the future.

Expectation in Ministry: Journals

One can readily see how a sense of expectation expands through this project. One of the exciting features and key for me was an invitation to each church to interface with the elders at Trinity Family Life Center (TFLC). The following schedule lists the meeting dates of the five participant pastors and their elders with TFLC elders. All dates are in 2014: Pastor Blue, April 21; Pastor Gray, May 12; Pastor Green, May 19; Pastor Brown, June 16; Pastor Black, June 21. The following is an entry from Pastor Green's journal:

> Six elders and I went to Pickerington to attend the elders' meeting at Pickerington. They were very excited to see the possibilities of what we might become, and they were nervous because they didn't know what to expect. The meeting went well. My elders were able to watch the Trinity elders minister to two individuals. My elders were impressed with how God spoke through the Trinity elders to the individuals. We talked about our experience all the way home. I had the Trinity elders anoint my elders and commission them for ministry at our church. Two of my elders were unable to attend. My elders are very excited to begin meeting with people. They were impressed with the amount of encouragement that flowed out of the Trinity elders. We decided to follow the same procedures the Trinity elders follow when meeting with people by standing when they enter, introducing ourselves, and waiting on God before speaking words of encouragement and sharing insight. We want to make sure that it is God speaking and not us. (May 19)

Pastor Blue records similar thoughts from his meeting at TFLC:

> Had a great trip over to Pickerington with 5 of the 6 elders from Grace. One of them was not able to go because of a last minute situation at work. I think our guys were eager to see what elders look like in action and I was anxious for them to experience it. Grace does not have the charismatic background that Trinity does, but I have been planting some seeds for it over the past three and one half years. I believe we are at a point that these elders can be a catalyst for growth in this area. [W]e had a good meeting and witnessed and heard what elder ministry was all about. Talked about[o]ur impressions on the way home. General excitement among all the men. The key question was: How are we going to get our people to buy into this? How will we get them to accept the offer to come and be prayed for? (April 21)

Another entry a few weeks later from Pastor Blue: "Regular weekly meeting tonight. Revisited chapters 1–3 of Lowery [a second book I assigned for study: *Walking in the Supernatural* by R. L. Lowery]. Good discussion and much excitement about seeing God do miraculous things at Grace" (June 2). Pastor Gray records his meeting with the elders of TFLC: "Met with elders' team at Trinity this month to discuss how they run their elders team. It was both encouraging and challenging. We see great value in the elders of the church being a safe-haven and security blanket to the church for prayer and ministry" (March 16). The impact of visually observing a seasoned team of elders in context can prove to be very valuable.

Expectation in Ministry: Exit Interviews

When I asked Pastor Green's head elder to say a few words concerning his experience in this project, he said that the ministry of elders has been "vital, and I think it will bring into the church things it has not had, such as authority, such as taking charge over bad things that happen, things like that." When asked if he would be willing to be a part of a team to go out and promote elders ministry on a broad basis, Pastor Brown said, "I would be honored to be part of a team." He continued, "I was so excited to see our elders team up with some other folks, bragging about the Lord Jesus Christ.…"

Pastor Gray observed a special insight in his experience, having just planted a church in the near past: "These men are going to carry the load so people in the church will be conditioned to the fact that they can come…to a team of men to help create a culture for help, when I don't have to be the one and only minister."

And finally Pastor Black, who is sixty-six years old and facing retirement, said: "I also see these guys being important in pastoral transition. The timing on this thing is really, really perfect." This is significant for the researcher's point of view, because the pastor who followed me at TFLC after thirty-eight years of ministry will confirm that the elders were the key component in a very difficult transition in pastoral ministry.

Anointing in Ministry (ANT): Pre-test/Post-test

Questions 9 and 10 looked at the ability of the pastor to hear, learn, and follow the Word of God through study and prayer. These elements are so important that the apostles appointed other men to a "servant ministry" so they would have time for both of these vital elements in Christian ministry (see Acts 6:2–4). Question 9 probes the all-important grounding in the Word of God and the ability to teach it (1 Tim. 3:2; Titus 1:9). All five pastors record their answers as "very confident" in this vital area of ministry. Scripture connotes a valuable anointing to those who excel in the Word of God (1 Jn. 2:27). See Figure 5.9:

Figure 5.9: Confident in grounding in the Word of God and the ability to teach it

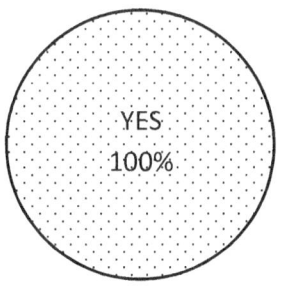

Five Pastors

Question 10 relates directly to the prayer life. Traditionally, if one is being honest, the prayer life becomes a causality to a busy ministry schedule. Three of the five pastors admitted to spending less than adequate time in prayer. Only Pastor Green and Pastor Blue were very confident in their prayer life. There is an anointing that comes through prayer, as Jesus's life demonstrates. Pastor Black shared a valuable insight here: his intention was to "use the elder board as a means to hold me accountable and help in spiritual formation. This will prove very valuable." See Figure 5.10:

Figure 5.10: Spending less than adequate time in prayer

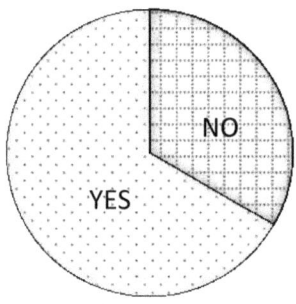

Five Pastors

Anointing in Ministry: Journals

As stated above in its description, the anointing involves "hearing" and "doing," a characteristic MO of Jesus (Jn. 5:19–20). For example, Pastor Green records the following:

> Tonight we had our first visitors to the elder team. A young man with his parents and sister came for prayer before he headed off to work at a summer camp. I felt very proud as I watched the elders welcome this family and pray, not only for the young man, but also for his family. They spoke amazing words of encouragement into him and he received it. Before the evening was over, the entire family was in tears as they experienced God's love in the room through the elders. After

the family left, the elders talked about the experience. They were excited! They knew that this is what it was all about. They left that evening very encouraged and fulfilled. (May 29)

Pastor Brown's elders were so excited they went out into the neighborhood seeking ministry: "Today at 7pm, two teams of CL's [elders] went out into the neighborhood to knock on doors and minister to the people. Brother Bell from Zion went with them. They came back with great testimonies of the faithfulness of God [including miraculous healing testimonies] — July 23."

Pastor Gray experiences the anointing in a situation of spiritual warfare. He writes:

> Tonight our elder team was called upon to go minister to a tragic situation in our community. Five days ago a 15-year-old girl committed suicide in her parents' basement. She attended my son's junior high school. Her mother called our church and explained that their entire family was being tormented, could not sleep and were sensing evil in their home. We spent one and a half hours at their Pickerington home counseling, casting out spirits and anointing each doorway with oil. It was heavy, but very effective. (May 15)

Again a similar entry with Pastor Gray on June 9: "We received a request by a core family in the church to come pray over their home. They stated that they are seeing things at night and the kids are having night terrors. We prayed over their home and gave them scriptures to do battle with in the future."

Finally, Pastor Blue records an interesting event with the elders of his church and their ability to step out in faith:

> Had invited our Lead Team chair and his wife to come for prayer and encouragement. After conversation we prayed for them and the Holy Spirit brought forth a prophetic word of encouragement for them. After praying for them I asked if anyone had a word or picture God was showing them and a couple of the elders spoke out. So, they are already willing to take some risks and allow gifts to be activated.

The above testimony picks up one of our subthemes of praying in the supernatural using prophetic manifestations. The pattern of more and more faith being released the longer the elders operate and feel their way into the giftings is evidenced throughout the journals. I see no regression as to boldness or gifting in the timeline of the journals.

Anointing in Ministry: Exit Interviews

Here Pastor Blue commented: "Some of our elders just individually take it upon themselves to pray for folks about the needs of the body. This group just begins to pray boldly for folks and that is just awesome." When speaking about a group of men who meet regularly for accountability and prayer, Pastor Black's head elder said: "We have thousands of pastors that do not have that piece in place, and you know when you have people praying for you to make such a difference, that's fantastic." To this statement Pastor Black added: "They just need to sound off and share and to have someone they can trust because there are just so many deep things a pastor has and he has to get it off his chest. This becomes a good and manageable thing where we really get to know each other."

Humility (HUM): Pre-test/Post-test

Question 15 reveals the characteristic of humility throughout the pastoral responses of the post-test questionnaire. I believe humility to be perhaps the most strategic characteristic in the entire elder template. When asked "How have your elders helped you fulfil your pastoral calling," three of them said they felt a measurable presence of personal support through wise counsel to the pastor as well as emotional/prayer encouragement. See Figure 5.11:

Figure 5.11: Sensed personal support of elders

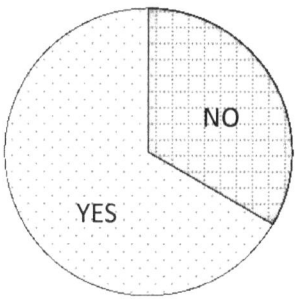

Five Pastors

Pastor Brown mentions the help he received in carrying the pastoral care load of the church. For a pastor to admit and appreciate these "helps" is a true sign of humility. Pastor Green commented: "They bring me more peace of mind knowing that they are available and support me. I love having a group of men who support me in prayer and practice. It has been amazing!"

Humility: Journals

As previously stated, the writer believes that humility is the defining characteristic in an elder program. One of the core scriptures in this project is 1 Peter 5:1–5. Peter records in verse 5: "Likewise you that are younger be subject to the elders. Clothe yourselves, all of you, with humility toward one another, for God opposes the proud, but gives grace to the humble." Martin Luther said, "I am more afraid of pope 'self' than of the pope in Rome and all his cardinals."[257] Proverbs 16:18 reminds us, "Pride

---

[257] Wayne A. Mack, *Humility: The Forgotten Virtue* (Phillipsburg, NJ: P & R Publishing Co., 2005), 10.

goes before destruction and a haughty spirit before a fall." And finally, William Farley reminds us of the emphasis of scripture on this issue. Scripture says:

> God esteems the humble (Isa. 66:2).
>
> He dwells with the contrite and lowly (Isa. 57:15).
>
> He blesses the poor in spirit (Matt. 5:3).
>
> He graces the humble (James 5:6).
>
> He guides and teaches the humble (Ps. 25:9).
>
> He regards the lowly (Ps. 138:6).[258]

Brother Farley continues: "The bottom line is this; the indispensable virtue, the one needed for intimacy with God and all spiritual fruitfulness, is humility—what Jesus also called being 'poor in spirit' (Matt. 5:3). About this virtue and its importance I was relatively ignorant."[259]

In our study, Pastor Green continues to record instance after instance of this most blessed characteristic demonstrated in his elders in response to their invitation to serve:

> Feb. 24—I received a response from Mike this afternoon. He was very surprised that I asked him and did not feel adequate to the task.
>
> Feb. 27—Mike humbly accepted the position, again expressing his surprise.
>
> March 7—Dave accepted the invitation by E-Mail. He expressed that he was humbled by the invitation.
>
> March 24—This was our first official elders meeting. Two of the three men did not know each other. They all expressed their shock when asked to join the team. What a wonderful group of humble men.

---

[258] William P. Farley, *Gospel Powered Humility*, (Phillipsburg, NJ: P & R Publishing Co., 2011), 2.
[259] Farley, *Gospel Powered*, 23.

Later that evening Pastor Green recorded: "During our prayer time, I was moved to tears. What an incredible experience praying with such Godly men! The room was filled with the presence of God."

> April 3—Mike and John both accepted the invitation. They were surprised to be asked and humbly accepted. Again I was overwhelmed with tears as we prayed together. I felt so honored to be able to pray with such Godly men. They too felt the presence of the Lord.
>
> April 10—I also asked Rick on the same Sunday. He was very surprised and didn't know what to say. I believe these are the right men for the team. Again I was moved emotionally when praying.
>
> April 17—Rick and Mike both accepted the invitation to join the team. Rick was extremely humbled by the invitation.

Pastor Blue records on May 5: "The elders continue to be excited about the possibilities for this ministry. All are realizing the importance of it and are ready to embrace the responsibility. Some are already experiencing spiritual warfare. I am more impressed every time I meet with these guys over their maturity, purity, strength, wisdom and humility. This is going to be a great thing for the church."

Pastor Black records on May 29: "I am in prayer for the group that will meet tonight. I am already eager for this group which is a good thing. My life seems to be so out of order for a number of reasons; health, church, retirement. I will be seeking clarifying prayer tonight." These entries are quite moving for me to review. They cause me to remember my own journey, as it was unfolding.

Humility: Exit Interviews

When asked, "What has it been like to share with other men on this level?" Pastor Green's head elder responded: "That has probably been the best part. As Pastor said we take it as important, yet I would use a different word because I see how solemn it is, so we see it as very serious, as in now let's examine our lives and make sure we stay committed to the cause that we have been called to."

When asking Pastor Blue what it has been like going through this process, he responded: "The biggest thing was trusting, rather than going through the names that they thought would make good elders. We had to trust that discernment [of the congregation]. And it was really neat to see the folks that the congregation responded to, people that I said, 'Oh yeah, I didn't think about that person for whatever reason.'"

Concerning the project in general, Pastor Brown added: "Now to see that as a pastor I don't know how excited one is to be, but I am highly excited about it. So I think it is a process that is just started and we are committed to seeing it through. It is a huge blessing, and thanks for involving us."

Pastor Gray said, "I don't have to be the one and only minister. I don't have all the answers, that we all have gifts, and I don't have to be the one and only minister."

Finally, Pastor Black said he was uptight about trusting the process to the congregation but admits, "If I were handpicking the board it would not look like it looks today. So instead I trusted the process."

The data suggests a real growth curve in faith and trusting on the part of all of these pastors who have been in ministry for many years and yet have never walked down this road before.

Outcomes

I begin by saying a word concerning the reversal of emphasis in the data categories originally sought to be measured by the project. These consisted of salvation, healing, deliverance, and prayer counseling. These four constitute the central parameters of human need in ministry to individuals or couples by the elders. The problems and challenges of the human race at its core are rooted in our opaque relationship with God and our interminable sinfulness (Ps. 51:5; Rom. 3:23, 5:10). When one applies the blood and merit of Jesus Christ's sacrifice for our bondage in life, whatever that bondage may be, one truly is transferred from one realm to another (Acts 26:18). This then becomes a natural outworking (process) of eldership in the ministry of the local church (James 5:14).

However, when placing the original data categories in the abstract, I relied on my experience with a seasoned group of elders who had developed their ministry protocol over many years of experience together as a group. I failed to realize that a new group of elders would most likely not be proficient in these ministries because they would be feeling their way into unchartered territory. Based on the data received in this project, there is no doubt in my mind that the participant church elders will become proficient in these four data categories as time elapses. The readings assigned (especially R. L. Lowery) for study under the direction of the participating pastors will ensure this outcome. Nevertheless, it will take time for the participant groups to feel their way into the ministry of the supernatural. Having said this, I will concentrate on the primary results of the data source inquiry concerning CM, EXP, ANT, and HUM, respectively. For herein, the results of this project begin to shine.

To begin with, even though the elders did not yield sufficient experience to become proficient in the four original data strategies of salvation, healing, deliverance, and prayer counseling, 100 percent of them did register confidence in administering salvation and healing for the future, and 80 percent were confident as to their ability to administer deliverance and prayer counseling as the ministry unfolds. Fortunately, I picked seasoned pastors for this project, and 80 percent of them were very confident to step into supernatural ministry in the days ahead. However, 40 percent were concerned about the ability of the congregation to understand the breadth of the ministry and adapt to it successfully.

In the category of EXP, 100 percent of the participant pastors were relieved to have help in sharing the ministry load in the local church. As recorded earlier, this carries with it a "great relief" both mentally and physically, considering the demands of modern life. Eighty percent expected their elders to exhibit spiritual growth, partially because of a deliberate discipleship regimen and partly because of the asset of progressive accountability within the members of the group. Pastor Black specifically mentioned this component in his analysis. Sixty percent of the pastors acknowledged the benefit of ongoing training, including a revisit to the home church elders at some point in the future. The data indicates a growing expectation of the ministry of elders into the future.

In the area of ANT, 100 percent of the participants registered positive thoughts concerning their knowledge of the Word of God and teaching it to others. Since the Word of God is the foundation of the church, at least in the Methodist tradition (Wesley & Sola Scriptura), its understanding and application to everyday life remains vital. Sixty percent of the pastors admitted to spending less than adequate time in prayer, and yet 40 percent were very confident in their present prayer life.

Concerning the area of HUM, 60 percent of the participant pastors felt a measurable presence of personal support and encouragement. They loved having the prayer support from a seasoned group of men. Virtually 100 percent of the participants discerned a kind of "corporate companion" in the ministry of Biblical Eldership. As Pastor Green so aptly put it, "They bring me more peace of mind knowing that they are available and support me. I love having a group of men support me in prayer and practice."

Finally, 80 percent of the participant pastors experienced supernatural gifts in operation within the group at some point in the process. Only Pastor Black failed to report any supernatural incidents; however, in his behalf, he already had existing groups trained to minister in all four areas tagged in the original abstract. The need was being met.

I believe the data indicate the elders' project to be a huge success, measuring ministry outcomes in a completely new context for virtually all the participants. I believe the days ahead for these participant churches will be significant because the number—not only of the churches, but of the communities at large—will touch on a level of Christ's love and wholeness desperately needed in a modern, secular post-Christian culture.

6

Reflection, Summary and Conclusion

Reflection

ELDERS MAY PROVE TO BE an orderly, efficient, and effective way to manage pastoral administration in the local church in the twenty-first century. As we have seen, the flowering of the importance and utilization of the lay person, developed under John Wesley and the Methodist movement, is a well-documented phenomenon. It has been the position of this paper in part, that the seeds of ecclesiastical reform are firmly embedded in the Wesleyan Movement.

I am arguing for an ancient form of ministry adapted to a modern context; it still has validity. We see this in the worldwide international athletic contest known as the Olympics. We see it in the neo-religious sect known as the Masons, based out of an ancient platform. With this, much of the current literature in local Christian mission is reexamining the entire meaning of what it means to be an apostolic church today with its antecedent leadership known as elders. The data indicate that a simple New Testament structure, Spirit-guided and charismatically gifted, will do wonders for the ministry of the average pastor in the local church. If one needs a theological category in which to place this structure, the priesthood of the believer is appropriate.

We have piled on century after century of a graduated leadership pattern of bishop, elder, and deacon until the church's orthopraxis has become unrecognizable from the New Testament witness. As a result of the present study, the data seem to suggest that the treatment of this subject of Biblical Eldership could provide an intervening variable in the solution to the problematic high causality rate in Christian ministry. Even though most all the pastors who participated in this study already had positive ministries, the insertion of Elders Ministry supplied a well-needed component for an overall congregational hermeneutic of spiritual oversight and supervision wedded to a supernatural charismatic framework.

With respect to the name of elder, it is used interchangeably in the New Testament with other terms as bishop, overseer, and presbyter. The same could be said with being a follower of Jesus. One could be called a Christian, a believer, a follower of the Way, a disciple of Jesus, or a Jesus follower. In fact, all of these terms are used on a regular basis in the public vernacular. Even though the author's denomination (UMC) has designated a term to primarily mean one thing (elder), it does not preclude it from meaning something quite similar. However, selling it to the hierarchy may be another matter.

In our society and in much of our thinking in America, we have pushed "elders" to the margins. We warehouse them; we stick them in nursing homes because they have outlived their usefulness, sideline them, and generally pass them by. Once past a certain age, a person has broken through an age barrier in the mind of the culture. However, elders are still important and have something to offer. God would gather the discarded and those pushed to the margins rather than consign them to the realms of endless monotony. We should still tap this segment of the Body of Christ because the Spirit of God places value in what they have to offer. For our purpose here, elders have not only earned seniority, but qualify for a dimension of leadership that is Spirit-empowered and vital to congregational health. The author's project will give elders that opportunity and may just unlock a treasure trove of wisdom and revelation in the house of God.

A significant benefit of Biblical Eldership is that it will easily fit into any structure of church polity. One does not have to alter the local church structure to accommodate the Elders Ministry as conceived herein. This could prove a positive aspect for pastors who would have a more difficult time convincing their people of a more aggressive change in policy. After the ministry of elders is in place, the congregation will see quickly the benefit of the design for the larger congregation. The data clearly suggest this trend.

In addition, the more the pastor recruits the input of the congregation to this process early on, the better will be the overall response of the church to the ongoing effectiveness of the ministry. Ownership is always an important ingredient to positive forward movement.

Summary

The purpose of this project was to develop and test a template for raising up local church eldership and its implication for charismatic ministry in the local church. Primary Christian behaviors involving supernatural ministry were connected to the ability of elders to function effectively. These behaviors were

Christian conversion, physical healing, deliverance, and prayer counseling. In addition, auxiliary areas of development also of interest included but were not limited to anointing in ministry, humility, confidence in ministry, and a greater expectance that real needs in the body of the congregation would be met by a functioning elders' ministry.

I chose a qualitative framework for this study because the qualitative design is poised to give "multiple forms of data"[260] which then allow a researcher to "review the data, make sense of it, and organize it into categories or themes that cut across all of the data sources."[261] This approach works well with the grounded theory design (also employed), since the grounded theory method allows the categories to come up out of the data, making it plain for tabulation.

In this study, I chose three methods of data collection, familiar of course to this kind of sociological research and effective in their results to complete the process of methodological triangulation. The three methods were a comparison of a pre-test and post-test questionnaire, participant journals, and recorded summary exit interviews with each of the five pastors involved in the study. On the post-test questionnaire, four out of five additional Likert-style questions were administered to measure quality and effectiveness of the project. Again, those results are seen in chapter 5, page 128.

I also chose a broad demographic spread for the five pastors, including racial, ethnic, and age variables. This allowed me to surmise whether the template developed for the project would be broad enough for multiple variations in future congregations interested in the study. Having experienced the power of Biblical Eldership in my church, I anticipated a similar result in the

---

[260] Creswell, *Research Design*, 185.
[261] Creswell, *Research Design*, 186.

churches being studied. Since the attempt of the entire project has been to be as faithful to the scriptures and the leading of the Holy Spirit as possible, I admit along with the Apostle Paul that "our competence is from God" (2 Cor. 3:5). Any and all continuing benefits from the present project go to God and God alone.

I have been interested in the overall big picture effect that elders' ministry has had on the local churches. Have the pastors been encouraged after having been surrounded by elders who desire to grow in discipleship? Have the congregations seen fruit from the ministry; have the elders themselves grown in spirituality and ministry effectiveness, including moving in the gifts of the Spirit, especially the prophetic? Has there been an overall positive forward movement for the advancement of the Kingdom of God for the churches? With the present template in tow, these and other questions have yielded positive results.

The unfolding progression of this study is thematic in origin and reflected in the beginning outline. First, in chapter one I developed my focus in ministry, in which I merged a spiritual autobiography with my context in ministry, locating myself in a traditional denominational setting. The context in ministry includes an explanation as to how this project emerged in the local context.

Secondly, I delineated the basic theological positions taken in scholarship relative to elders' ministry over the last seventy-five years, contrasting viewpoints with the present practice of Biblical Eldership as determined in this thesis. Points of agreement and disagreement are noted in the review.

Thirdly, the theoretical foundation for the ministry of Biblical Eldership is examined, studying both Old Testament and New Testament sources. Historical examples are given from the first four centuries of the church, tracking the migration of the concept of eldership ministry in this most formative period of the church. Finally, the study argues, theologically, for a return to a simple New Testament design in Biblical Eldership involving recruitment, training, apprenticeship, and mobilization of the elders' ministry.

Fourthly, I analyze the methodology used in the study. The research design and validity for triangulation were set in place. In this setting, the role of the researcher was discussed, along with the study's hypothesis, measurement parameters, and instrumentation used in the project.

Fifthly, I laid out the evidence to substantiate this hypothesis. This information was taken directly from the field experience of the pastors in their local context. Herein, demographics as well as analysis of the raw data were categorized, while themes emerged from the data. The themes were then given specific findings where outcomes were summarized. Comparisons were drawn from the data, locating each church's experience before and after the initiation of Biblical Eldership. Graphs are located to visually substantiate the findings.

Finally, in the last chapter of the document, the author's reflections on the project and its implications for the future are given, along with the formal summary of the project. Concluding, I recommend topics for further study and follow-up for Elders Ministry. The reader is left with a few parting comments concluding with the future of Elders Ministry in the Body of Christ and the UMC. The horizon holds promise for all who dare to journey.

Conclusion

Reflecting back on this study, I have very positive feelings about the process and the outcome of the project. As stated earlier, the plight of pastors has been on the researcher's heart for many years. Having preached in multiple churches all across the country, I have seen from firsthand experience the desperation which is embedded in the experiences of pastoring a local church in America. Seminaries have not always adequately prepared pastors for what they will face in the local church. Denominational judicatories have not always supported pastors in the difficult dance of moving congregations forward as they experience resistance from entrenched church members bent on keeping the status quo. Pastors are left to "figure it out" as they go, knowing that their livelihood is always on the line.

I hope that the initiation of an Elders Ministry as designated in the current study may supply a needed and positive step forward for pastors in the field who feel isolated, frustrated, and alone.[262]

In today's church culture, the concept and job description of elder varies from church to church. Each congregation adopts their own concept and functionality based on their grasp of the scriptures and their church structure. As a result, the concept of elder covers a spectrum from co-pastor to deacon to board member to trustee as well as additional points in between. The present project is meant to help bring clarity to a concept originally embedded in scripture and still useful for today's experience.

In the present template, as spiritual overseers the elders will naturally become more involved in the day-to-day issues. They will tend to connect with the members more intimately and bring to the pastor's attention major issues for consideration. As such, they will be able to minister more closely to families and

---

[262] "The Mayo Clinic warns that those in so-called 'helping professions' are high-risk candidates for burnout, because such people identify so strongly with their work that they tend to lack a reasonable balance between work life and personal life and try to be everything to everyone. This sounds like a lot of pastors I know.'" Jared C. Wilson, *The Pastor's Justification: Applying the Work of Christ in Your Life and Ministry* (Wheaton, IL: Crossway Books, 2013), 18.

members since they feel responsible for their spiritual welfare. This in turn will tend to release more accountability on the part of the leadership to the concerns of the larger congregation while everyone feels a part of the process. Eldership could also provide a greater safeguard for the pastor, since the elders are more likely to see and hear what is going on from the congregation's perspective. These steps will advance the overall ministry on a positive footing.

Two items for further study should be noted at this time. First, a further study of the import of women into elders' ministry would be helpful for the overall concept in the local church. In the UMC, female elders have been a part of the clergy for many years. Congregations may expect some female leadership among the elders if they were to be commissioned. Female leadership could also impinge on the dynamics in the overall administration of Elders Ministry in the local congregation. Scripture both in the Old and the New Testaments reveal male elders in the leadership sequence. The insertion of female elders would be a helpful study.

Secondly, I recommend further study on Biblical Eldership in the UMC. Points of clarification would center around how Biblical Eldership may affect the larger system of local church administration. In addition, the concept of "first among equals" may need some additional clarification within the UMC structure because the pastor in our system is already designated and ordained to elder. There may be significant resistance to the intrusion of a "rival elders program" in a system that already provides elders. The onus would be on justifying additional elders from the perspective of the hierarchy of the church.

The present template for Elders Ministry is obviously a grassroots initiative in the local congregation based on a perceived need for heightened spiritual leadership in the local church. Whether or not it would become an "official" part of the UMC Judicatory is another question indeed. However, based on the data from the present study, I am convinced that Biblical Eldership is a concept whose time has come. Pastors and leaders who discern the importance of a spiritual leadership construct based on a New Testament design will indeed profit from this new paradigm. The entire Methodist system sprang from such a design. God only knows if it can happen again for the twenty-first-century church.

Appendix A

Demographics Survey

Dear Brothers, in preparation for our meeting on March 27 @ 1pm, Trinity Family Life Ctr. I would very much appreciate if you could fill out the following Demographic and church Intake questions for my project. This will allow me to have a composite view of each church. Please bring the completed form with you to the meeting. Many thanks. STK

Size of Congregation

Average Attendance

Congregational Demographic: rural, County seat, Urban, suburban, college or university?

Age of the Pastor

Education of the Pastor (last degree)

Experience of the Pastor in Ministry?

Theological ideological of the Pastor

Theological ideology of the congregation

Church budget

Congregational distinctives?

Gender patterns in discipleship?

Is the church a staff guided church? Please list staff positions.

Schedule of services

Is it a cell based congregation?

Goals and expectations presented at the last Congregation Meeting or Charge Conference

Are there regular prayer/intercessory groups which meet?

Approximate number of volunteers?

Are there any community agencies using your building?

Are there any long or short range plans anticipated

How many postal zones do your draw from?

What are your financial stewardship expectations (every-member canvass)?

Founding date of congregation?

Appendix B

Pre-Test Questionnaire

Elders Ministry Project: Pre-Questionnaire

1. How do you plan to function as the senior leader with a group of elders in the days ahead?

2. This project will measure four primary areas: salvation, healing, deliverance, and prayer counseling. How will this ministry behavior affect your church and life?

3. Do you feel confident in leading people to a "saving knowledge" of Jesus Christ and to pray for their salvation? [explain]

4. As people may demonstrate aberrant behavioral patterns, how confident do you feel in the ministry of deliverance?

5. Have you ever engaged in "prayer counseling" (inner healing/James 5:16) with other persons in need?

6. What spiritual gifts are most dominant in your Christian walk?

7. What are your feelings concerning Elders Ministry and moving in the miraculous?

8. In thinking about your "preferred future" of Elders Ministry in your local church, what areas of equipping would be most helpful to you?

9. Elders are to know and teach the Word of God (Acts 20:20). How confident do you feel in this role?

10. Where are you in your prayer life and how can it be improved?

11. What kinds of benefits do you anticipate in the development of Elders Ministry in your church?

12. What kind of challenges do you anticipate in developing this ministry?

13. What will be the "growing edge" (learning curve) for you as you lead an Elders Ministry in your church?

14. What "concerns" do you have as you begin this process of developing and Elders Ministry in your church?

Appendix C

Post-Test Questionnaire

Elders Ministry Project: Post-Questionnaire

1. How do you plan to function as the senior leader with a group of elders in the days ahead?

2. This project will measure four primary areas: salvation, healing, deliverance, and prayer counseling. How will this ministry behavior affect your church and life?

3. Do you feel confident in leading people to a "saving knowledge" of Jesus Christ and to pray for their salvation? [explain]

4. As people may demonstrate aberrant behavioral patterns, how confident do you feel in the ministry of deliverance?

5. Have you ever engaged in "prayer counseling" (inner healing/James 5:16) with other persons in need?

6. What spiritual gifts are most dominant in your Christian walk?

7. What are your feelings concerning Elders Ministry and moving in the miraculous?

8. In thinking about your "preferred future" of Elders Ministry in your local church, what areas of equipping would be most helpful to you?

9. Elders are to know and teach the Word of God (Acts 20:20). How confident do you feel in this role?

10. Where are you in your prayer life and how can it be improved?

11. What kinds of benefits do you anticipate in the development of Elders Ministry in your church?

12. What kind of challenges do you anticipate in developing this ministry?

13. What will be the "growing edge" (learning curve) for you as you lead an Elders Ministry in your church?

14. What "concerns" do you have as you begin this process of developing and Elders Ministry in your church?

15. How have your elders influenced your ability to fulfil your pastoral calling in the local church?

16. On a scale of 1---5, five being the most desirable, how have your elders functioned in the spiritual administration of the church? (Please elaborate)

17. On a scale of 1---5, five being the most desirable, how have the spiritual loves of the elders themselves been affected by their experience? (Please elaborate)

18. On a scale of 1---5, five being the most desirable, how have your elders developed in their own spiritual gifting's (charismata)?

19. On a scale of 1---5, five being the most desirable, what kind of reception has your congregation given to the "elders ministry" up to this point in time? (Please elaborate)

20. What is the one significant "take-away" for you as the lead pastor concerning elder's ministry

Appendix D

Confidentiality Form

Informed Consent Form

Doctor of Ministry Project for United Theological Seminary

TITLE OF STUDY: Raising Up Biblical Eldership

RESEARCHER: Scott Kelso

INTRODUCTION

I understand that I have been asked to participate in a study about Raising up Biblical Eldership and its Implications for Charismatic Ministry in the Local Church.

INFORMATION ABOUT THE STUDY

I will be asked to:

1. Complete a written survey
2. Log a personal journal during the next five months related to my experience
3. Coordinate and interview process with the researcher and one elder
4. Visit on site, an Elder leadership team meeting on a Monday

180 Biblical Eldership

    Evening at Trinity FLC

5. Conduct an on-site interview with Scott Kelso and my new elder team at some point

During the focus group or any personal interviews an audio recording may be used to help accurately record data.

Risks and Benefits

I understand that the study involves the following benefits and/or risks:

Benefits: Possible increased awareness of the Holy Spirit personally and corporately and possibly a sense of increased unity among the elders of my church and the wider church fellowship in general.

Risks: No known risks are involved with participation in this study.

Confidentiality

It has been explained to me that the information I provide will be kept confidential. Data will be stored securely and will be made available only to persons conducting this study. No reference will be made in oral or written reports which could link me to the study. Your name and personal identify will not be associated specifically with any of the data gathered for this project.

Any recorded audio will be disposed of following the completion of the study. Transcripts will remain on file for 10 years.

Voluntary Participation

I understand that my participation in this study is voluntary. I may decline to participate without any penalty. If I decide to participate, I may withdraw from the study at anytime without penalty. Likewise, my participation may be terminated by the researcher without regard to my consent.

Contact Information

If I have any questions about the study, about my rights as a participant in the study, or experience any unusual or unexpected discomfort from participating in this study, I may contact: The researcher – Scott Kelso: stkelso@gmail.com or by phone at 614.348.4913 or the researcher's mentor at United Theological Seminary jruthven1@united.edu

Consent

When I sign my name, this means that I agree to participate in this study, that all of my questions have been answered, and that I am at least 18 years old. I have also been given a copy of this form.

Name_____   Date: _____
(Print)

Signature:_____

Appendix E

Project Invitation Letter

November 4, 2013

Dear Pastors,

I wish to thank and congratulate each one of you for your participation in my D.Min. Ministry project: "Raising Up Biblical Elders and Its Implication for Charismatic Ministry in the Local Church." The next twelve months will prove very exciting as you watch your local church go deeper in its experience of discipleship and ministry in the local church.

A plausible protocol for this process would include the following: a) between now and the end of the year meet with your SPRC and ask for their blessing on this project. Feel free to extract any of the information I have given you to this point so that they are fully informed. This will provide official cover for your project; b) at some point in early January, preach on Numbers 11, with emphasis on elders' ministry. Include an index card for each person in attendance to write one name on the card as a suggestion of a person who they feel would be elder qualified to serve with you in this ministry; c) appoint your first elder by the end of January

184 Biblical Eldership

from the names suggested and begin to pray and fast together for wisdom to add to the group. Accordingly, you and your first elder will appoint two more to join the group. Following an appropriate amount of time the now four members of elders will again suggest two additional until you have filled the group with your desired number of elders.

Additional information on elder's ministry will be provided as we move into the months ahead. We will all grow together as the Lord of the church works through our elders to bless the local ministry through spiritual supervision of the congregation, prayer, and ministry opportunities. I pray many blessings to you in this process and again, thank you.

Sincerely In Christ,

Pastor Scott T. Kelso

Appendix F

Invitation Form Letter

April 24, 2002

Name and Address

Dear

Our elders are presently in the process of extending an "invitation" to a couple of men to become Elders here at Trinity. We feel a need to increase our numbers. At out last meeting it was unanimous that you should be given an invitation.

The group is not a committee, but is seen as spiritual leaders for the purpose of oversight and ministry in this local church. We urge all Elders to aspire to the qualifications found in 1 Timothy 3:1-7 and Titus 1. I ask you to meditate on six aspects of manhood; moral, reputable, temperament, mature, disciplined, and ethical. In addition to the foregoing aspects of manhood, I believe these men should be men of prayer, spirit filled and able to move in ministry in the gifts of the Holy Spirit (1Cor.12:14). Also, they are required to be tithing members of this church.

186 Biblical Eldership

The basic responsibilities would be to attend the weekly meetings of our Elders on Monday evenings at 7pm, a monthly meeting with the Elders and wives for fellowship and prayer, and to be on call for pastoral ministry needs throughout the congregation as needed. Since your wife is an integral part of your life and witness, the both of you will want to earnestly seek God as to this calling to our church.

God bless you as you discern your commitment. Please let me know at your earliest convenience.

In Christ,

Pastor Scott

STK/lmk

One enclosure

Appendix G

Grace and Spirit Baptism

Prepared for
E 21 Scholars Consultation: London, England

May 6-7, 2016

Abstract

The New Covenant Spirit (Holy Spirit) which Jesus came to ratify on Calvary became a deposit (first fruits) of our inheritance of "all things" in Christ. At Pentecost, the Holy Spirit is seen as an "enclothing" of supernatural grace, empowering the individual believer, irrespective of status, to witness with supernatural giftings (charismata) while moving the Great Commission forward on earth. This first fruits promise is foreshadowed in the Old Testament (Is. 59:20-21); announced in the New Testament (Matt. 3:11; Mk.1:8; Lk.3:16; and John 1:33); received at Pentecost (Acts 2:39), and confirmed in the infant church (2Cor.3:2-3); resulting in a sequential and thematic coherence in mission throughout the ages.

Certainly the subject before us has been thoroughly investigated and I do not purport to bring any new revelation to the fore on this subject. Mountains of material have been produced over the last century of Biblical Scholarship relative to the subject of Spirit-Baptism. However, through my recent doctoral program, I did gain new insight concerning the central work of the Holy Spirit in the New Covenant. As we proceed, I will attempt to unpack some of these new insights in our presentation.

The title of our doctoral track was "A New Hermeneutic of Emphasis---Where Will It Lead Us? The Biblical and Practical Role of the Holy Spirit: Power and Gifts in Fully Proclaiming the Gospel." As Christians we understand that Jesus is the key link in all of salvation history. He is the divine link between the Father and the Spirit. He remains the bridge between God and man. In the Old Covenant, this bridge functioned as the written scripture (Torah); "a kind of guardian/ instructor (Gr. *paidagogas*, lit., child-leader) to take us to Christ and faith…"[263] (Gal. 3:24-25) "The written scripture could act only as a mirror---to show our dirty faces (our sin), but it didn't actually wash our faces!"[264] "By contrast, the New Covenant Spirit, that now indwells us, not only guides us as to the content of God's will but also motivates us to do it."[265]

All of this is of prime importance because the New Covenant Spirit (Spirit-Baptism) is what Jesus came to inaugurate and ratify through His death and resurrection (Jer. 31:31f; Ezek. 36:26). This New Covenant Spirit—the Holy Spirit—Jesus promised (Acts 1:4); Joel foretold (Joel 2:28-29); and Peter confirmed through Isaiah (59:20-21) and declared on the day of Pentecost (Acts 2:39). The Spirit would function as a first-fruits, a guarantee, a deposit on our inheritance of all that is to come

---

[263] John Mark Ruthven, *What's Wrong with Protestant Theology: Tradition vs. Biblical Emphasis* (Tulsa, OK, Word & Spirit Press, 2013), 133.
[264] Ibid.
[265] Ibid.

(Eph. 1:14; 2 Cor. 1:22, 5:5; Acts 20:32). Indeed, the Holy Spirit in us acts as a kind of "eminent domain" of His presence informing all that we do and think. In addition, in the big picture scene, Jesus' death and resurrection is His gift to the world, but the Baptism in the Holy Spirit is His gift to the church. Peter Hocken, an eminent Catholic priest and theologian says concerning the Baptism in the Holy Spirit: "Baptism in the Holy Spirit is the foundational grace of the Pentecostal and Charismatic movements as a whole."[266] Hocken goes on to say there is an objective character to the Baptism in the Holy Spirit from which the charisms mentioned in 1 Cor. 12:8-10 provide clear witness.[267] Because of this, the Baptism in the Holy Spirit is more than a subjective state and is clear that it serves as a gift (grace) for the church at large.

What is the Baptism in the Holy Spirit?

Concerning the Gospels and the Book of Acts, it was the understanding of the New Testament writers---especially Luke, that the seminal work of Jesus following His ascension was the sending of the Holy Spirit upon the waiting church for empowerment and mission. (Acts 1:8) Without this critical stage in the *ordo salutis,* (the sequence of salvation that ends up in Heaven), the church would be relegated to a ministry of "remembrance" only, being devoid of the power to confront the waiting world. Luke tells us that Jesus gave specific instruction to the disciples; "And behold, I send the promise of my Father upon you; but stay in the city, until you are clothed with power from on high." (Lk. 24:49) 'The coming of the Spirit in terms of an "enclothing" is found both in the Old Testament and in early

---

[266] Peter Hocken, *Azusa, Rome, and Zion: Pentecostal Faith, Catholic Reform, and Jewish Roots* (Eugene, OR, Pickwick Publications, 2016), 66.
[267] Ibid.

Christian thought."[268] As the 120 waited on the promise, the opportunity arrived on the day of Pentecost; a national festival gathering in Jerusalem for maximum effect. (Acts 2:1-4)

As with most seasons where "God is on the move" in the earth, there are those who are disinterested or not looking for the prophetic fulfilment of scripture. One can see them in Acts 2:12 where they exclaimed; "And all were amazed and perplexed saying to one another; what does this mean?" However, there were also those on the right side of history, Peter among them, who said:

> Men of Judea and all who dwell in Jerusalem, let this be known to you, and give ear to my words. For these men are not drunk, as you suppose, since it is only the third hour of the day; but this is what was spoken by the prophet Joel: 'And in the last days, it shall be, God declares, that I will pour out my Spirit upon all flesh, and your sons and your daughters shall prophecy, and your young men shall see visions, and your old men shall dream dreams....'" (Acts 2:14-17)

A striking aspect for our purpose here is the response of the people once Peter unpacked this Old Testament verse. Acts 2:37 records, "Now when they heard this they were cut to the heart, and said to Peter and the rest of the apostles; Brethren what shall we do?" Every good preacher deserves a solid response tethered to the message of the hour. Peter certainly received his. Furthermore, as Peter gave instruction to them in verse 38, conversion-initiation[269] took place and 3000 people were baptized in one day. Such would define a harvest in most anyone's book.

---

[268] See Judges 6:34; 1Chron.12:18; 2Chron.24:40; Judges 11:29, 13:24, 14:6, 19, 15:14. James D. G. Dunn, *Baptism in the Holy Spirit*, (Philadelphia, PA, The Westminster Press, 1970), 110.

[269] A term used throughout Professor James D. G. Dunn's work signifying the change that took place upon believing on Christ as Savior and Lord.

However, the point I wish to establish in this paper rests in verse 39: "For the promise is to you and to your children and to all that are afar off, everyone whom the Lord our God calls to him." This is a direct promise from Isaiah 59:20-21, echoed by Ezekiel 11:26; 37:14; 39:29; and Jeremiah 31:33. These scriptures are pregnant with the prophetic hope of the New Covenant Spirit promised by Jesus. Even the Apostle Paul sees this fulfilled in the New Covenant Spirit. (2 Cor. 3:2-3) As professor Jon Ruthven says; "it is clear from scripture that the essence of the New Covenant is the presence of the communicating, prophetic Spirit in our heart."[270] (Is. 59:21 > Acts 2:39)

Ministry Under the Anointing of the Baptism in the Holy Spirit

Following Pentecost, it was a whole new day for the people of God. They began to "hear" and "do", a kind of show and tell ministry (Lk. 24:19; Ro. 15:18; Heb. 2:4), which overturned the ancient world. As people were introduced to the Christian Gospel, they encountered the faith in a kind of "multi-image (video) platform, as opposed to a single-image (one dimensional/picture) platform. The presentation of the gospel was dynamic and alive with signs following. Consider these scriptures that offer an accurate overview of ministry related activity under this new anointing.

- 2 Cor.12:12: "The signs of a true apostle were performed among you in all patience, with sign and wonders and mighty words."
- Heb. 2:3b-4: "It was declared at first by the Lord, and it was attested to us by those who heard him, while god also bore witness by signs and wonders and various

---

[270] Ruthven, Lectures, Fall, 2013, United Theological Seminary, Dayton, Ohio.

- miracles and by gifts of the Holy Spirit distributed according to his own will."

- Gal. 3:5: "Does he who supplies the Spirit to you and works miracles among you do so by works of the law, or by hearing with faith?"

- 1 Cor. 2:4-5: "and my speech and my message were not in plausible words of wisdom, but in demonstration of the Spirit and power, that your faith might not rest in the wisdom of men but in the power of God."

- 1 Thess. 1:5: "for our gospel came to you not only in word, but also in power and in the Holy Spirit and with full conviction."

- Ro. 15:18-19: "For I will not venture to speak of anything except what Christ has wrought through me to win obedience from the Gentiles, by word and deed, by the power of signs and wonders, by the power of the Holy Spirit, so that from Jerusalem and as far round as Illyricum I have fully preached the gospel of Christ."

- Eph. 1:19: "and what is the immeasurable greatness of his power in us who believe, according to the working of his great might...."

- 1 Cor. 4:20: "For the kingdom of God does not consist in talk but in power."

- 1 Pet. 4:6: "For this is why the gospel was preached even to the dead, that though judged in the flesh like men, they might live in the spirit like God."

- Lk. 24:49: "And behold, I send the promise of my Father upon you; but stay in the city, until you are clothed with power from on high."

Herein we are not only looking at what the Bible says, but also what it emphasizes. How do we determine emphasis? By such things as repetition, amount of space devoted, summary statements, statements of importance, correlation of themes e.g. spirit to prophecy; salvation to healing; faith to miracle.[271] In addition, a review of the above scriptures reminds the student of the New Testament, that one cannot divorce the Apostle Paul's theology from his experience. For example; two words that Paul uses side by side and at times interchangeably are Spirit *(pneuma)* and grace *(charis)*. Since our theme is "Grace and Spirit Baptism," it is incumbent for us to detail these two words.

Spirit *(pneuma)* and Grace *(charis)* Briefly Considered

Professor James D.G. Dunn has written extensively on the themes of Jesus and the Spirit. With respect to these two words, Gr. *pneuma* and *charis*, a clear theme emerges from Paul's use of the terms in the New Testament. Dr. Dunn, in his book Jesus and the Spirit, begins a section on Spirit and Grace by saying: "Spirit *(pneuma)* for Paul is essentially an experiential concept; by that I mean a concept whose content and significance is determined to a decisive degree by his experience."[272] This is confirmed (through repetition and the amount of space devoted) by reading the following passages: Ro. 5:5; 6:1f; 8:9, 14: 1 Cor. 1:4-9; 6:9-11, 12:13; 2 Cor. 1:21f; Gal. 3:1-5; 4:6f; Col. 2; 11f: 1Thess.1:5; Titus 3:5-7. Professor Dunn continues: "For the moment it is enough that the experiential dimension of Paul's spirit talk be recognized as a basic fact of his whole religion and theology."[273] We see in this for Paul that the inner life of the Spirit of God supersedes all

---

[271] Ibid.
[272] James D. G. Dunn, *Jesus and the Spirit: A Study of the Religious and Charismatic Experience of Jesus and the First Christians as Reflected in the New Testament* (Grand Rapids, MI, William B. Eerdmans Publishing Company, 1975), 201.
[273] Ibid., 202.

ritual and outward requirements of faith. (Ro. 2:8f; 2 Cor. 3; Gal. 4:6; Phil. 3:3; Eph. 1; 7f) In fact, "the Spirit is that power which transforms a man from the inside out, so that metaphors of cleansing and consecration become matters of actual experience in daily living. (1 Cor. 6:6-11).[274] Since the Holy Spirit is a person, Paul's experience correlates with a "lived relationship" in the third person of the Trinity, an experience mirrored by Jesus at His baptism.

Secondly, the word *grace (charis)* unfolds in two aspects. First, it betrays the salvation event which is an act of "wholly unmerited generosity on God's part."[275] The Cross is God's eschatological deed! And secondly, grace for Paul is the grace of conversion establishing a living relationship with the living God. (Ro. 3:24; 5:15; 17:20; 1 Cor. 1:4f; 15:10; 2 Cor. 6:1; Gal. 1:6, 15; 2:21; Eph. 2:5-8.) Again, for Paul "grace is not something merely believed in but something experienced,"[276] resulting in a transforming power, "a continuing experience of a relationship with God sustained by divine power." (Ro. 5:2; Col. 3:16).[277] In fact, the word *grace* literally means "generous empowerment." This means, for instance, that even Paul's greetings and benedictions at the beginning and end of his letters are not just formality but the most sincere wish "that they experience grace afresh with the power of God existentially moving in and upon their lives."[278] In a real sense, these become "code words" respecting the "normative life in the Spirit in their respective Christian communities."[279] The "grace ("generous, charismatic empowering") and "peace" ("wholeness, health, balance,

---

[274] Ibid., 201.
[275] Ibid., 202.
[276] Ibid., 202.
[277] Ibid., 203
[278] Ibid.
[279] Ruthven, *What's Wrong*, 164.

harmony") are ways of focusing on the Holy Spirit, which in our present era is the essential operating principle of the church and the Christian Life."[280]

In addition, the concept of "charisma" is a concept which we owe almost entirely to Paul.[281] "Being a distinctively Pauline word, of the 17 occurrences in the New Testament, only one comes from outside the Pauline corpus, and that from a typically Pauline passage (1 Peter 4:10)."[282] Dr. Dunn goes on to say: "Josephus does not use the word at all, and there are only two occurrences in Philo."[283] It is therefore significant that Paul's choice of this word betrays his own experience and his understanding of how God relates to man in the work of the Cross and Resurrection.

In summary, we see a consistency of thought and experience even overlapping one another in the use of these words in Paul's letters. This is seen in Romans 1:11 where Paul says: "For I long to see you, that I may impart to you some spiritual gift *(pneumatikon* qualifies *charisma),*[284] "underlining Paul's conscious dependence on the Spirit and grace for any benefit he can bring to the believers at Rome."[285] All of this spiritual power is reinforced with the Baptism in the Holy Spirit, placing the disciple in an ongoing, dependent, lived relationship with the Third Person of the Trinity.

---

[280] Ibid., 163. See: 2 Cor. 1:11-12; 9:14; Eph. 1:16-17; 6:18-19; Phil. 1:4:6-7 (peace = Spirit); Col. 1:3-4 (faith); 1:9; 4:3-4; 1 Thess. 1:2-5; esp. 1 Thess. 3:10; 5:17-20; esp. 2 Thess. 1:11; 3:1; 1 Tim.4:5-6; Phlm. 5-6; cf. Rom. 15:29.
[281] Dunn, *Jesus and the Spirit*, 205.
[282] Ibid.
[283] Ibid., 206.
[284] Dunn, *Jesus and the Spirit*, 208.
[285] Ibid.

The Transformation of the Ancient World

With this spiritual dynamic in tow, the church grew exponentially not only in numbers, but in power as well, (Acts 2:41, 4:4; 4:7; 5:14; 6:7; 8:12; 9:31) passing on the faith effectively and consistently. By the beginning of the second century it was obvious that Jesus was not coming back as soon as originally anticipated. Furthermore, frontiers were opening up to the East, the North, and the South. While the church was dutifully settling in the cities of Jerusalem, Antioch, and Alexandria, the mission emphasis of Acts 1:8 lay before them as the specter of virgin territory welcomed their witness. With this growth, a Spirit-baptized constituency toppled the ancient world. Professor Ramsey MacMullen in his book *Christianizing the Roman Empire A.D. 100-400* gives a convincing case historically that Christianity displaced the competing religions of the day as well as the Roman stronghold itself. One must acknowledge that this was done essentially through the early church's moving in signs, wonders, and deliverance ministry. Professor MacMullen says, "Within the first three centuries, [the church] had successfully displaced or superseded the other religions of the empire's population."[286] An amazing feat as he continues; "Among all the leisurely great developments, this one of the period A.D. 100-400 might fairly be given pride of place in the whole of Western history."[287] In other words, the establishment of Christianity as the central faith of the ancient world gets first place in the pursuit of the living God.

By the end of the fourth century, a 7000-mile oval church belt had been established in the Mediterranean from Rome in the

---

[286] Ramsey MacMullen, *Christianizing the Roman Empire* A.D. *100–400*, (New Haven, CT, Yale University Press, 1984), viii.
[287] Ibid.

North to Alexandria in the South. This was accomplished with no printing press, no church buildings, and no banks to loan money while crossing language, cultural and ethnic barriers at every turn. The faith that was "once delivered to the saints," was getting serious traction. A Spirit-baptized church moving in the "charismata" (gifts of grace) released a spiritual persona that was in many cases irreducible in the ancient world. Hence, the greater works that Jesus promised (Jn. 14:12) were being manifest.

In effect, Jesus Himself admitted that the church would eventually outshine His own ministry in a prophetic sense. The three years of ministry by Jesus prior to Pentecost were but a "sampling" of all that was to come after Pentecost. Yes, Jesus spoke to large crowds, but many left unconvinced or unwilling to change. His upbraiding of the cities of Chorazin, Bethsaida, and Capernaum was due to their lack of response to his "mighty works" performed in their midst. (Matt. 11:20-24) Additionally, Jesus' lament over Jerusalem signifies their refusal to repent as well. He concluded: "Behold, your house is forsaken and desolate." This is hardly the resonance of a successful ministry. Even at the end the crowds rejected Him and yelled "crucify Him." The largest group to witness Him in a post-resurrection appearance was 500 and only 120 waited on the blessed promised Holy Spirit prior to Pentecost. Yes, he touched some individuals and turned their world upside down, but He was crucified and buried under a brutal Roman regime on the backside of the world, having never traveled over 100 miles from his birthplace and leaving no written record of His life and works.

However, because Jesus said; "I will go to the Father…," we the church would be destined for greater things. These greater things began at Pentecost with the Baptism in the Holy Spirit. Following this event, the number of people eligible for a faith fueled life swelled exponentially as mentioned above. These were the "greater things" as the Spirit of God, through the church, conquered the ancient world. As a result, even the Apostles admitted; "From now on, therefore, we regard no one from a human point of view; even though we once regarded Christ from a human point of view, we regard him thus no longer." (2 Cor. 5:16)

From a pastoral perspective one question a leader may ask is how broad is the current Pentecostal movement embracing the Baptism in the Holy Spirit? We know for a fact, the movement is no flash in the pan. For over 100 years it has swept people of faith to a higher plane, resulting in the largest single segment of the Body of Christ throughout the world, some 600,000,000. For those who are not in this flow of the Holy Spirit, perhaps a second look would be in order.

Following a thorough analysis of the world Christian scene going into the 21st century, Alister McGrath, in his book *The Future of Christianity*, predicts only three segments of the Body of Christ will flourish in the 21st century. They are the Roman Catholic Church, the Eastern Orthodox Church, and those churches tethered to the Pentecostal/Charismatic wing of the church.[288] Particularly with respect to the latter, "Pentecostalism stresses a direct, immediate experience of God and avoids the rather dry and cerebral forms of Christianity which many find unattractive and unintelligible."[289] "In addition, the movement uses a language and form of communication which enable it to bridge cultural gaps highly effectively."[290] And as Harvey Cox has said, "With Pentecostalism, the marginalized and

---

[288] Alister McGrath, *The Future of Christianity*, (Oxford, England, Blackwell Publishing, 2002), 106.
[289] Ibid.
[290] Ibid.

disadvantaged have found a second and relevant home."[291] Since Asia, Africa, and the Global South are aflame with Spirit-filled Christianity and are highly represented by the poor, this seems to be a good fit for the end-times church.

Into the 21st Century

The 20th century was marked by an amazing outpouring of the Holy Spirit and God's grace. With it we witnessed the Azusa Street Revival, the Healing Revival with William Branham, Oral Roberts, et.al, the Latter Rain Movement of 1948 with George Hawtin and the Sharon Orphanage and School in North Battleford, Saskatchewan, Canada, the Charismatic Movement with Dennis Bennett and the American Episcopal Church, the Catholic Charismatic Renewal launched at Duquesne University, the Third Wave Movement under John Wimber and the Vineyard Church, the Toronto World Outpouring at the Airport Vineyard Church in Toronto under John Arnott, and more. All of these movements had as their core, the Baptism in the Holy Spirit and the practical dissemination of the gifts (charismata) of the Spirit for the whole church, not to mention the whole area of Pentecostal/Charismatic worship, "drawing from the divine treasury things new and old: new in their expression, old in their inner life and significance."[292]

It has been said that the Charismatic Renewal movement in the United States was really the first nation-wide revival in history. This is because the First and Second Great Awakenings

---

[291] Harvey Cox, *Fire from Heaven: The Rise of Pentecostal Spirituality and the Reshaping of Religion in the Twenty-First Century*, (Reading, MA, Addison-Wesley Publishing, 1995), 107.

[292] Peter Hocken, (*The Glory and the Shame: Reflections on the 20th Century Outpouring of the Holy Spirit*), Surrey, England, Eagle-Guildford Publishing, 1994), 102.

had affected only the Protestant sector of the church and not all of them. But the Charismatic Renewal touched the full range of Protestant churches as well as the Roman Catholic Church and the Eastern Orthodox Church. Henry Lederle says, in his excellent book *Theology with Spirit,* "For the first time in Christian history, all the major branches of Christianity albeit to differing extents, were influenced globally by the same religious awakening or renewal movement."[293] Similarly, Dr. Peter Hocken, speaking to the Charismatic Leaders Fellowship in 2012, said concerning the Renewal: it "was a huge joy for Catholics and Protestants to find that for the first time they were part of the same tide of the Spirit and were able to experience a real communion in the Holy Spirit with each other. This outpouring of the Spirit was profoundly transforming and life giving."[294] As Father Hocken has said, "Catholics and Protestants have received the same gift."[295] A theological challenge (for some), is "the claim that the basic spiritual reality being called the baptism in the Spirit is fundamentally the same grace across all different church groupings impacted by the Charismatic movement."[296] Hocken concludes: "The church needs such movements to shake it up, to challenge all forms of immobility and stagnation, and to unleash fresh dynamism from the Spirit of God."[297] This ecumenical thrust has been and remains one of the big stories of the renewal movement.

For those who can remember or who were in attendance, the visible and organic unity in which the harmony of the Body of

---

[293] Henry I Lederle, *Theology with Spirit: The Future of the Pentecostal & Charismatic Movements in the 21st Century,* (Tulsa, OK, Word and Spirit Press, 2010), 109.

[294] Peter Hocken, *Notes,* @ CLF meeting in Regent University, February, 2012.

[295] Peter Hocken, *Azusa, Rome,* 67.

[296] Ibid. 76.

[297] Ibid., 107.

Christ was on display for the entire world to see took place in New Orleans at an ecumenical Spirit-filled conference at the Superdome in 1987, with 60,000 in attendance, 30,000 of which were Roman Catholics. Of this event Peter Hocken said, "The Body of Christ in North America had been given a unity or a communion at the level of the Spirit which became a spring board for the task of achieving a unity at the level of the mind (articulated faith), leading to a level of embodied community."[298]

For the past twenty years I have been privileged to be a part of the Charismatic Leaders Fellowship (CLF), made up of top-tier leadership from the four streams of the faith: Catholic, Protestant, Non-denominational, and Pentecostal. I presently serve as Chairman of the group, succeeding our immediate past president, Francis MacNutt. The group has benefited from scholars of the renewal such as Dr. David DuPlesis, Dr. Vinson Synan, Dr. Larry Christensen, Dr. Francis MacNutt, Dr. Everett Fullum, Dr. Kevin Ranaghan, et al. In addition, we have within our ranks such Apostles as Dr. Ken Sumrall (deceased), Mateo Callisi, Dr. Randy Clark, Dr. Billy Wilson, Rev. Gerald Derstine, and others.

The CLF was originally convened by Dennis Bennett in Seattle in 1971 as the Charismatic Concerns Committee. The group was commissioned, firstly, to solve various problems attached to the burgeoning Charismatic Renewal. For example, group exorcism, with little or no follow up, or believers' baptism vs. infant baptism. Our group made it possible for Charismatic leaders from different traditions, who previously didn't know each other, to meet and to come to esteem one another and to build relationship which led them to address various problems like the ones just mentioned. In order to facilitate such an important

---

[298] Peter Hocken, *Notes,* @ CLF meeting in Regent University, February, 2012.

good, the meetings were by "invitation only," and because the meetings were off the record, no recordings of any kind were permitted. In this, the participants were able to freely speak when controversial issues came up for discussion and prayer.

The group eventually moved to the Marianist Apostolic Center in Glenco, MO, and became known as the "Glenco Group." Over the years the group became a catalyst for other important meetings, such as the North American Renewal Service Committee (NARSC), sponsoring large ecumenical gatherings held in Kansas City, New Orleans, St. Louis, San Antonio, Indianapolis, and Orlando. Through the decades of the 1980's and 1990's, thousands attended these gatherings as the group gave focus to the growing Charismatic Renewal.

The most famous of these ecumenical meetings was held in 1977 at Kansas City with 40,000 people in Arrowhead Stadium. Reflecting on this conference during the last night of the event, Fr. Michale Scanlan, a Catholic leader in the renewal said: "There is going to be a new and more powerful ecumenical leadership in unity of Christian life than we have seen in the last five hundred years. And that's going to come from this conference, and its going to be the most important fruit of the whole conference."[299] In addition, most all of the mainline denominations birthed renewal movements in their respective streams in the wake of the Kansas City Conference. Our United Methodist conference known as Aldersgate Renewal Ministries is still going strong with several thousand in attendance each summer.

---

[299] David Manuel, *Like a Mighty River: A Personal Account of the Charismatic Conference of 1977*, (Orleans, MA, Rock Harbor Press, 1977), 205.

Concluding Thoughts

As the God parent of the Kansas City Conference, the CLF has a unique place in the world-wide renewal movement. What was suggested by Father Scanlan has become visible in the work of the CLF and beyond. Presently we are forming an effective mixture of the wisdom of age and experience accomplished by including early renewal leaders as well as a growing number of current generation and next-gen leaders from the U.S. and around the world. The Charismatic Leaders Fellowship has been and continues to be a powerful tool of the Holy Spirit for promoting unity, reconciliation, and evangelism to the world today. Scholars, leaders, and next-gen voices converge at strategic cities around the world to give strategy for the final day's harvest. As we move into the future, the greatest convergence of Spirit-filled Christians in history will "set the table" for the coming of our Lord Jesus Christ. The future looks replete with opportunities for ecumenical courage as the Pentecostal/Charismatic streams within Christianity coalesce. As we move deeper into the "last days" mentality, it will take the whole church presenting the whole Gospel to the whole world. Then perhaps Matthew 24:14 will finally be realized.

Bibliography

Abraham, William J. *Crossing the Threshold of Divine Revelation.* Grand Rapids, MI: Eerdmans, 2006.

Adams, Jay. *A Call to Discernment: Distinguishing Truth from Error in Today's Church.* Eugene, OR: Harvest House Publishers, 1987.

Aikman, Davie. *One Nation without God.* Grand Rapids, MI: Baker Books, 2012.

Aitken, Ellen Bradshaw. "To Remember the Lord Jesus: Leadership and Memory in the New Testament." *Anglican Theological Review* 91, no. 1 (2009): 31-46.

Alexander, Paul. *Signs & Wonders: Why Pentecostalism Is the World's Fastest Growing Faith.* San Francisco, CA: Jossey-Bass, 2009.

Arias, Mortimer. *Announcing the Reign of God: Evangelization and the Subversive Memory of Jesus.* Eugene, OR: Wipf & Stock Publishers, 1984.

Ashbrook, R. Thomas. *Mansions of the Heart: Exploring the Seven Stages of Spiritual Growth.* San Francisco, CA: Jossey-Bass, 2009.

Ashley, Timothy R. *The Book of Numbers:* NICOT. Grand Rapids, MI: Wm. B. Eerdmans Publishing Co., 1993.

Bainton, Roland H. *Here I Stand: A Life of Martin Luther.* Nashville, TN: Abingdon-Cokesbury Press, 1950.

Bank, Robert J. *Paul's Idea of Community: The Early House Churches in Their Cultural Setting.* Revised Edition. Grand Rapids, MI: Baker Academic, 1994.

Barclay, William. *The Letter to the Ephesians: Daily Study Bible Series.* Philadelphia, PA: The Westminster Press, 1975.

Barna, George. *Future Cast.* Austin, TX: Barna/Tyndale House Publishers Inc., 2011.

Bernard, Daniel. *The Church at Its Best: God's People Empowered, Unified, and Mobilized for Their Community.* Mobile, AL: Evergreen Press, 2008.

Billman, Frank H. *The Supernatural Thread in Methodism: Signs and Wonders among Methodists Then and Now.* Lake Mary, FL: Creation House Press, 2013.

Braaten, Carl E., and Robert W. Jensen, eds. *The Strange New World of the Gospel: Re-Evangelizing in the Postmodern World.* Grand Rapids, MI: Eerdmans, 2002.

Bridges, Jerry. *The Transforming Power of the Gospel.* Colorado Springs, CO: NaviPress, 2012.

Brown, Michael L. *Authentic Fire: A Response to John MacArthur's Strange Fire.* Lake Mary, FL: Excel Publishers, 2014.

_____. *Hyper-Grace: Exposing the Dangers of the Modern Grace Message.* Lake Mary, FL: Charisma House, 2014.

Brown, Raymond. "*Episkope* and *Episkopos*: The New Testament Evidence." *Interface* 1, no. 2 (Spring 1979): 322-338.

Bruce, F. F. *Answers to Questions.* Grand Rapids, MI: Zondervan Publishing, 1972.

_____. *New Testament History.* New York, NY: Anchor Books, Doubleday & Company, 1969.

_____. *The Message of the New Testament.* Grand Rapids, MI: Eerdmans, 1972.

_____. *The Spreading Flame.* Grand Rapids, MI: Eerdmans, 1958.

Calvin, John. *Commentary on the Harmony of the Pentateuch, Vol. 4.* London, England: Calvin Translation Society, 1845.

Campbell, Alastair. *The Elders.* Edinburg Scotland: T & T Clark, 1974.

Carnell, E.J. *The Case for Biblical Christianity: Essays on theology, philosophy, ethics, ecumenism, fundamentalism, separatism.* William B. Eerdmans Publishing Company, 1969.

Clark, Randy. *Supernatural Missions: The Impact of the Supernatural on World Missions.* Mechanicsburg, PA: Global Awakening, 2012.

_____. *There Is More: Reclaiming the Power of Impartation.* Mechanicsburg, PA: Global Awakening, 2006.

Coffman, Elesha J. *The Christian Century & the Rise of the Protestant Mainline.* New York, NY: Oxford University Press, 2013.

Cole, Neil. *Church 3.0.* San Francisco, CA: Jossey-Bass, 2010.

_____. *Organic Church: Growing Faith Where Life Happens.* San Francisco, CA: Jossey-Bass, 2005.

_____. *Primal Fire: Reigniting the Church with the Five Gifts of Jesus.* Bonita Springs, FL: Tyndale Momentum, 2012.

Collins, Kenneth J. *The Evangelical Moment: The Promise of an American Religion.* Grand Rapids, MI: Baker Academic, 2005.

Colson, Charles. *Kingdoms in Conflict: An Insider's Challenging View of Politics, Power, and the Pulpit.* Grand Rapids, MI: William Morrow/Zondervan Publishing House, 1987.

Conner, Kevin S. *The Church in the New Testament.* Portland, OR: City Bible Publishing, 1982.

Coppedge, Allan. *The Biblical Principles of Discipleship.* Grand Rapids, MI: Zondervan/Francis Asbury Press, 1989.

Cotton, Roger D. "The Pentecostal Significance of Numbers 11." *Journal of Pentecostal Theology* 10, no. 1 (2001): 3-10.

Coulter, Dale M. "Christ, the Spirit, and Vocation: Initial Reflections on a Pentecostal Ecclesiology." *Pro Ecclesia* 9, no. 3 (2001): 318-339.

Cox, Harvey. *Fire from Heaven: The Rise of Pentecostal Spirituality and the Reshaping of Religion in the Twenty-first Century.* Reading, PA: Addison-Wesley, 1995.

_____. *The Future of Faith.* New York, NY: Harper Collins, 2009.

Creswell, John W. *Research Design; Qualitative, Quantitative and*

Mixed Methods Approaches. Thousand Oaks, CA: SAGE Publications, 2014.

Dayton, Donald W. *Theological Roots of Pentecostalism*. Grand Rapids, MI: Eerdmans, 1987.

DeArteaga, William. *Forging a Renewed Hebraic and Pauline Christianity*. forthcoming.

DeTochville, Alexis. *Democracy in America, Vols. 1 and 2*. New Rochelle, NY: Arlington House Publishers, Classics of Conservatism, 1840.

Dever, Mark. *Nine Marks of a Healthy Church*. Wheaton, IL: Crossway Books, 2000.

DeYong, Kevin. *Taking God at His Word: Why the Bible is Knowable, Necessary, and Enough, and What that Means for You and Me*. Wheaton, IL: Crossway Books, 2014.

Dickerson, John S. *The Great Evangelical Recession*. Grand Rapids, MI: Baker Books, 2013.

Diprose, Ronald. *Israel and the Church: The Origin and Effects of Replacement Theology*. Rome, Italy: Instituto Biblical Evangelica Italiano, 2004.

Douthat, Ross. *Bad Religion: How We Became A Nation of Heretics*. New York, NY: Free Press, 2012.

Doyle, Sir Arthur Conan. *The Complete Sherlock Holmes, Vol. I*. New York, NY: Barnes & Noble, Signature Edition, Sterling Publishing Inc., 2012.

Durant, Will. *The Story of Civilization IV: The Age of Faith*. New York, NY: Simon and Schuster, 1950.

Dyke, Drew. *Yawning at Tigers: You Can't Tame God, So Stop Trying*. Nashville, TN: Thomas Nelson, 2014.

Elliott, John H. "Elders as Honored Household Heads and Not Holders of 'Office' in Earliest Christianity." *Biblical Theological Bulletin: A Journal of Bible and Theology* 33, no. 2 (2003): 77-82.

_____. "Elders as Leaders in 1 Peter and the Early Church." *Currents in Theology and Mission* 28, no. 6 (2001): 549-559.

Enslin, Morton Scott. *Christian Beginnings: Part I and II.* New York, NY: Harper Torch Books, 1956.

Farley, William P. *Outrageous Mercy: Rediscovering the Radical Nature of the Cross.* Phillipsburg, NJ: P & R Publishing, 2004.

_____. *Gospel Powered Humility.* Phillipsburg, NJ: P & R Publishing, 2014.

Farr, Thomas F. *World of Faith and Freedom: Why International Religious Liberty Is Vital to American National Security.* New York, NY: Oxford University Press, 2008.

Fee, Gordon D. "Reflections on Church Order in the Pastoral Epistles, with Further Reflection on the Hermeneutics of AD Hoc Documents." *Journal of the Evangelical Society* 28, no.2 (1985): 146.

Ferguson, Charles W. *Organizing to Beat the Devil: Methodists and the Making of America.* Garden City, NY: Doubleday & Company, 1971.

Finke, Roger, and Rodney Stark. *The Churching of America, 1776–2005: Winners and Losers in Our Religious Economy.* New Brunswick, NJ: Rutgers University Press, 2011.

Franke, John R. "Origen: Friend or Foe?" *Christianity History Magazine* 22, no. 4 (2003): 18-23.

Freeman, Charles. *A New History of Early Christianity.* New Haven, CT: Yale University Press, 2009.

Galli, Mark, and Ted Olsen, eds. *131 Christians Everyone Should Know.* Nashville, TN: Broadman and Holman Publishers, 2000.

Garofalo, Steven. *Right for You, but Not for Me: A Response to Moral Relativism.* Charlotte, NC: Triedstone Publishing Co., 2013.

Gelpi, Donald L. *Pentecostalism: A Theological Viewpoint.* New York, NY: Paulist Press, 1991.

Gertz, Steven. "Opponents of Allegory," *Christian History Magazine,* Issue 80, Vol.22, no.4: 28-29.

Getz, Gene A. *Elders and Leaders: God's Plan for Leading the Church.*

Chicago, IL: Moody Publishers, 2003.

Gilmore, James H., and B. Joseph Pine II. *Authenticity: What Consumers Really Want.* Boston, MA: Harvard Business School, 2008.

Gordon, Bruce. *Calvin.* New Haven, CT: Yale University Press, 2009.

Grady, J. Lee. *10 Lies the Church Tells Women.* Lake Mary, FL: Creation House Publishers, 2000.

Gray, Joan S. *Spiritual Leadership for Church Officers.* Louisville, KY: Geneva Press, 2009.

Green, Joel B., and David F. Watson, eds. *Wesley, Wesleyans and Reading Bible as Scripture.* Waco, TX: Baylor University Press, 2012.

Greig, Gary S., and Kevin Springer, eds. *The Kingdom and the Power: A Biblical Look at How to Bring the Gospel to the World with Power.* Ventura, CA: Regal Books, 1993.

Grudem, Wayne. *Systematic Theology: An Introduction to Biblical Doctrine.* Grand Rapids, MI: Zondervan, 1994.

Guder, Darrell L., ed. *Missional Church: A Vision for the Sending of the Church in North America.* Grand Rapids, MI: Eerdmans, 1998.

Guenther, B., and D. Heidebrecht. "The Elusive Biblical Model of Leadership." *Direction* 28, no. 2 (1999): 153-165.

Guinness, Os. *The Global Public Square: Religious Freedom and the Making of a World Safe for Diversity.* Downers Grove, IL: IVP Books, 2013.

Guthrie, D., and J. P. Motzer. *The New Bible Commentary Revised.* Grand Rapids, MI: Eerdmans, 1970.

Hanson, Richard. *The Christian Priesthood Examined.* London, UK: Lutterworth Press, 1979.

Harkness, Georgia. *The Ministry of the Laity.* Nashville, TN: Abingdon Press, 1962.

Harris, Joshua, and Eve Stanford. *Humble Orthodoxy.* Colorado Springs, CO: Multnomah Books, 2013.

Hayford, Jack. *Living the Spirit Formed Life: Growing in the 10 Principles of Spirit-Filled Discipleship.* Ventura, CA: Regal/Gospel Light, 2001.

Hersh, Alan, and Tim Catchin. *The Permanent Revolution: Apostolic Imagination and Practice for the 21st Century Church.* San Francisco, CA: Jossey-Bass, 2012.

Hillerbrand, Hans J. *A New History of Christianity.* Nashville, TN: Abingdon Press, 2012.

Hocken, Peter, *Pentecost & Parousia: Charismatic Renewal Christian Unity, and the Coming Glory.* Eugene, OR: Wipf & Stock Publishers, 2013.

Hunsberger, George R., and Craig Van Gelder, eds. *The Church between Gospel and Culture: The Emerging Mission in North America.* Grand Rapids, MI: Eerdmans, 1996.

Hutmaker, Jim. *Interrupted: When Jesus Wrecks Your Comfortable Christianity.* Colorado Springs, CO: NaviPress, 2014.

Jefford, Clayton N. *Reading the Apostolic Fathers: A Students Introduction.* Grand Rapids: MI: Baker Academic, 2012.

Jenkins, Phillip. *The Next Christendom.* New York, NY: Oxford University Press, 2002.

Johnson, Bill, and Randy Clark. *The Essential Guide to Healing: Equipping All Christians to Pray for the Sick.* Minneapolis, MN: Chosen Books, 2011.

Johnston, Philip S. *The IVP Introduction to the Bible.* Downers Grove, IL: IVP Academic, 2006.

Keil, C. F., and Franz Delitzech. *Old Testament Commentaries, Vol. I.* Grand Rapids, MI: Associated Publishers and Authors, 1971.

Kelly, J.N.D. *Early Christian Doctrines.* New York, NY: Harper Collins Publishers, revised edition, 1978.

Kelso, Scott. *Ice on Fire: A New Day for the 21st Century Church.* Nashville, TN: Thomas Nelson Publishers, 2006.

_____. *Let's See What Sticks: Kingdom Living in Chaotic Times.* Enamclaw, WA: WinePress Publishing, 2013.

Kendall, R. T. *Holy Fire: A Balanced Biblical Look at the Holy Spirit's Work in Our Lives.* Lake Mary, FL: Charisma House, 2014.

Kraemer, Kendrik. *A Theology of the Laity.* Philadelphia, PA: The Westminster Press, 1958.

Kraft, Charles H. *Deep Wounds, Deep Healing: An Introduction to Deep-Level Healing.* Ventura, CA: Regal, 2010.

Lederle, Henry L. *Theology with Spirit.* Tulsa, Ok: Word and Spirit Press, 2012.

Lent, Gregory A., ed. *The Complete Biblical Library: Old Testament Study Bible in 22 Volumes: Deuteronomy.* Springfield, MO: World Library Press, 1995.

Levison, John R. "Prophecy in Ancient Israel: The Case of the Ecstatic Elders." *Catholic Biblical Quarterly* 65, no. 4 (2003): 503-521.

Logos Bible Software: "Introductory Note to the Epistle of Polycarp to the Philippians." In Roberts, A., J. Donaldson, and A. C. Coxe, eds., *The Ante-Nicene Fathers, Volume I: The Apostolic Fathers with Justin Martyr and Irenaeus,* Chapter XLVI. Buffalo, NY: Christian Literature Company, 1885.

_____. Clement of Rome. *The First Epistle of Clement to the Corinthians.* In Roberts, A., J. Donaldson, and A. C. Coxe, eds., *The Ante-Nicene Fathers, Volume I: The Apostolic Fathers with Justin Martyr and Irenaeus,* Chapter XLVI. Buffalo, NY: Christian Literature Company, 1885.

_____. "Introductory Note to the Works of Origen." In A. Roberts, J. Donaldson, and A.C. Coxe, eds., *The Ante-Nicene Gathers, Volume IV: Fathers of the Third Century: Tertullian, Part Fourth; Minucius Felix; Commodian, Origen, Parts First and Second.* Buffalo, NY: Christian Literature Company, 1885.

_____. *Origen against Celsus* F. Crombie, Trans. In A. Roberts, J. Donaldson, and A.C. Coxe, eds., *The Ante-Nicene Fathers, Volume IV: Fathers of the Third Century: Tertullian, Part Fourth; Minucius Felix; Commodian; Origen, Parts First and Second,* Chapter LXXV. Buffalo, NY: Christian Literature Co., 1885.

———. *The Epistle of Ploycarp to the Philippians.* In Roberts, A., J. Donaldson, and A. C. Coxe, eds., *The Ante-Nicene Fathers, Volume I: The Apostolic Fathers with Justin Martyr and Irenaeus, Chapter V.* Buffalo, NY: Christian Literature Crusade, 1885.

Lovelace, Richard F. *Dynamics of Spiritual Life: An Evangelical Theology of Renewal.* Downers Grove, IL: Inter-Varsity Press, 1979.

Lowery, T. L. *Walking in the Supernatural.* New Kensington, PA: Whitaker House, 2007.

Mack, Wayne A. *Humility; The Forgotten Virtue.* Phillipsburg, NJ; P & P Publishing Company, 2005.

MacMullen, Ramsay. *Christianizing the Roman Empire: A.D. 100–400.* New Haven, CT: Yale University Press, 1984.

MacNutt, Francis. *The Nearly Perfect Crime: How the Church Almost Killed the Ministry of Healing.* Grand Rapids, MI: Chosen Books, 2005.

Mangabrodi, Vishal. *The Book that Made Your World: How the Bible Created the Soul of Western Civilization.* Nashville, TN: Thomas Nelson, 2011.

Mann, Thomas. *The Oxford Guide to Library Research: How to Find Reliable Information Online and Offline.* New York, NY: Oxford University Press, 2005.

McGrath, Alister E. *Christian Theology: An Introduction.* 5th ed. Oxford, England: Wiley-Blackwell, 2011.

———, ed. *The Christian Theological Reader.* 4th ed. Oxford, England: Wiley-Blackwell, 2011.

———. *The Future of Christianity.* Oxford, England: Blackwell Publishing, 2002.

McIntosh, Doug. *The War within You: Overcoming the Obstacles to Godly Character.* Chicago, IL: Moody Press, 2001.

McManners, John, ed. *The Oxford Illustrated History of Christianity.* New York, NY: Oxford University Press, 1992.

McNeil, Reggie. *The Present Future: Six Tough Questions for the*

Church. San Francisco, CA: Jossey-Bass, 2003.

McNiff, Jean, and Jack Whitehead. *Your and Your Action Research Project*. 3rd ed. New York, NY: Routledge, 2010.

Miles, Matthew B., A. Michael Huberman and Johnny Saldana. *Qualitative Data Analysis: A Methods Sourcebook*. Los Angeles, CA: Sage Publications, 2014.

Miller, David W. "The Uniqueness of New Testament Church Eldership." *Grace Theological Journal* 6, no. 2 (1985): 315-327.

Milne, Garnet Howard. *The Westminster Confession of Faith and the Cessation of Spirit Revelation: The Majority Puritan Viewpoint on Whether Extra-Biblical Prophecy Is Still Possible*. Eugene, OR: Wipf & Stock, 2008.

Moody, Dale. *The Spirit of the Living God*. Philadelphia, PA: Westminster Press, 1968.

Morris, Robert. *The God I Never Knew: How Real Friendship with the Holy Spirit Can Change Your Life*. Colorado Springs, CO: WaterBrook Press, 2011.

Muthiah, Rob. "Charismatic Leadership in the Church: What the Apostle Paul Has to Say to Max Weber." *Journal of Religious Leadership* 9, no. 2 (2010): 7-26.

Myers, William R. *Research in Ministry: A Primer for the Doctor of Ministry Program*. Rev. ed. Chicago, IL: Sage Publications, 2000.

Newbegin, Leslie. *Foolishness to the Greeks: The Gospel and Western Culture*. Grand Rapids, MI: Eerdmans, 1986.

Newhaus, Richard J. *Doing Well and Doing Good*. New York, NY: Image Books, 2012.

Nichols, Stephen J. *Bonhoeffer on the Christian Life: From the Cross, For the World*. Wheaton, IL: Crossway Books, 2013.

Olson, Roger E. *Arminian Theology: Myths and Realities*. Downers Grove, IL: IVP Academic, 2006.

Otto, Rudolph. *The Idea of the Holy*. New York, NY: Oxford University Press, 1950.

Ortiz, Juan Carlos. *A Call to Discipleship*. Plainfield, NJ: Logos

International, 1975.

Packer, J. I. *Seeing God in the Dark: Unraveling the Mysteries of Holy Living.* Peabody, MA: Hendrickson Publishing, 1995.

Parrott, Rod. "New Testament Elders in Their Context." *Impact* 4, no. 1 (1980): 27-37.

Philip, James. *The Communicators Commentary: Numbers.* Edited by Lloyd J. Ogilvie. Waco, TX: Word Books, 1987.

Renfroe, Rob. *The Trouble with the Truth: Balancing Truth and Grace.* Nashville, TN: Abingdon Press, 2014.

Richardson, Alan. *A Theological Wordbook of the Bible.* New York, NY: The MacMillan Company, 1950.

_____. *An Introduction to the Theology of the New Testament.* New York, NY: Harper & Row Publishers, 1958.

Richardson, Cyril C. *Early Christian Fathers.* New York, NY: The Macmillan Company, 1970.

Roberts, J. W. "Eldership: The Rulership of Elders." *Firm Foundation* (March 25, 1958): 54-60.

Rorem, Paul. "Mission and Ministry in the Early Church: Bishop, Presbyters, Deacons." *Currents in Theology and Mission* 17, no. 1 (1990): 15-22.

Russell, Bob. *When God Builds a Church: 10 Principles for Growing a Dynamic Church.* West Monroe, LA: Howard Publishing, 2000.

Ruthven, Jon Mark. *On the Cessation of the Charismata: The Protestant Polemic on Post-Biblical Miracles.* Tulsa, OK: Word & Spirit Press, 2011.

_____. *What's Wrong with Protestant Theology? Tradition vs. Biblical Emphasis.* Tulsa, OK: Word & Spirit Press, 2013.

Rutz, James. *MegaShift.* Colorado Springs, CO: Empowerment Press, 2005.

Ryker, Philip Graham and Kent R. Hughes, eds. *Ecclesiastes.* Wheaton, IL: Crossway Books, 2010.

Schweizer, Eduard. *Church Order in the New Testament.* Eugene,

OR: Wipf & Stock Publishers, 1961.

Shibley, David. *Living as if Heaven Matters*. Lake Mary, FL: Charisma House, 2007.

Sidders, Greg. *The Invitation: The Not So Simple Truth about Following Jesus*. Grand Rapids, MI: Revell, 2011.

Sifton, Elisabeth, and Fritz Stem. *No Ordinary Men*. New York, NY: New York Review Books, 2013.

Sizemore, Bill. *The Fractured Church: Denominations and the Will of God*. Maitland, FL: Xulon Press, 2012.

Skarsaune, Oskar, and Reidar Hvalvik. *Jewish Believers in Jesus: The Early Centuries*. Peabody, MA: Hendrickson Publishers, 2007.

Smith, James Byron. *The Good and Beautiful God: Falling in Love with the God Jesus Knows*. Downers Grove, IL: IVP Books, 2009.

Snyder, Howard A. *Signs of the Spirit: How God Reshapes the Church*. Grand Rapids, MI: Academie Books-Zondervan, 1989.

Snyder, Howard A. *The Community of the King*. Downers Grove, IL: InterVaristy Press, 1977.

Strauch, Alexander. *Biblical Eldership: An Urgent Call to Restore Biblical Church Leadership*. Littleton, CO: Lewis & Roth Publishers, 1995.

Summerton, Neil. *A Noble Task; Eldership & Ministry in the Local Church*. Carlisle, UK: The Paternoster Press 1994.

Taylor, Charles. *A Secular Age*. Cambridge, MA: Belknap Howard, Harvard University Press, 2007.

Tertullian. *On Baptism*. In A. Roberts, J. Donaldson, and A.C. Coxe, eds., *The Ante-Nicene Fathers, Volume III: Latin Christianity: Its Founder, Tertullian* (Buffalo, NY: Christian Literature Company, 1885).

Thiselton, Anthony C. *The Holy Spirit – In Biblical Teaching through the Centuries and Today*. Grand Rapids, MI: Eerdmans, 2013.

Tiffany, Frederick C. and Sharon H. Ringe. *Biblical Interpretation: A Roadmap.* Nashville, TN: Abingdon, Press, 1996.

Thomas, Owen C. and Ellen K. Wondra. *Introduction to Theology*, 3rd ed. New York, NY: Morehouse Publishing, 2002.

Thorsen, Don. *Wesley and Calvin: Bringing Belief in Line with Practice.* Nashville, TN: Abingdon Press, 2013.

Van Gelder, Craig. *The Essence of the Church: A Community Created by the Spirit.* Grand Rapids, MI: Baker Publishing, 2000.

Virkler, Mark, and Patti Virkler. *Prayers that Heal the Heart: Prayer Counseling that Breaks Every Yoke.* Alachua, FL: Bridge-Logos, 2001.

_____. *Naturally Supernatural: Letting Jesus Live through You.* Camp Verde, AZ: Lamad Publishing, 2003.

Von Allmen, J.J., ed. *A Companion to the Bible.* New York, NY: Oxford University Press, 1958.

Von Campenhausen, Hans. *Ecclesiastical Authority and Spiritual Power in the Church of the First Three Centuries.* Peabody, MA: Hendrickson Publishing, 1997.

Wagner, C. Peter. *Acts of the Holy Spirit.* Ventura, CA: Regal Books, 2000.

Warkentin, Marjorie. *Ordination: A Biblical-Historical View.* Eugene, OR: Wiph & Stock, 1982.

Warren, Rick. *The Purpose Driven Church: Growth without Compromising Your Message and Mission.* Grand Rapids, MI: Zondervan Publishing, 1995.

Watson, David. *Called and Committed: World-Changing Discipleship.* Wheaton, IL: Harold Shaw Publishers, 1982.

Wesley, John. *The Works of John Wesley, Volume I*, 3rd ed. Grand Rapids, MI: Baker Book House, 1978.

_____. *The Works of John Wesley, Volume VII*, 3rd ed. Grand Rapids, MI: Baker Book House, 1978.

_____. *The Works of John Wesley, Volume VIII*, 3rd ed. Grand Rapids, MI: Baker Book House, 1978.

Wigger, John. *American Saint: Francis Asbury and the Methodists.* New York: NY: Oxford University Press, 2009.

Wiker, Benjamin. *Worshipping the State: How Liberalism Became Our State Religion.* Washington, D.C.: Regnery Publishing Inc., 2013.

Wilson, Jared C. *The Pastor's Justification: Applying the Work of Christ in Your Life and Ministry.* Wheaton, IL: crossway Books, 2013.

Wimber, John, and Kevin Springer. *Power Evangelism.* Ventura, CA: Regal Books, 2009.

Winslow, Paul, and Dorman Followwill. *The Lord & the Elders.* Hong Kong, China: New Life Literature Limited, 1999.

Wood, Lawrence W. *Pentecostal Grace.* Wilmore, KY: Francis Asbury Publishing Company, 1980.

_____. *The Meaning of Pentecost in Early Methodism: Rediscovering John Fletcher as John Wesley's Vindicator and Designated Successor.* Lanham, MD: The Scarecrow Press Inc. 2002.

Woolever, Cynthia, and Deborah Bruce. *A Field Guide to U.S. Congregations: Who's Going Where and Why.* Louisville/London, KY: Westminster/John Knox Press, 2007.

Wright, N. T. *How God Became King: The Forgotten Stories of the Gospels.* New York, NY: Harper One, Harper Collins, 2012.

Wright, Paul. *The Complete Biblical Library: Hebrews.* Springfield, MO: World Library Press, 1990.

www.ingramcontent.com/pod-product-compliance
Lightning Source LLC
Chambersburg PA
CBHW071611080526
44588CB00010B/1097